wrap *your* *heart* around it

A MEMOIR ABOUT LEARNING TO LOVE THE LIFE YOU HAVE

LynnMarie Rink

A POST HILL PRESS BOOK
ISBN (trade paperback): 978-1-61868-848-4
ISBN (eBook): 978-1-61868-849-1

WRAP YOUR HEART AROUND IT
A Memoir About Learning to Love the Life You Have
© 2016 by LynnMarie Rink
All Rights Reserved

Cover Artwork by Amy Slade
Cover Design by Quincy Alivio

Post Hill
PRESS

Post Hill Press
275 Madison Avenue, 14th Floor
New York, NY 10016
http://posthillpress.com

For all the lost and lonely souls. May you find your way home.

Acknowledgements

To Kathy Zamejc Vogt: Twenty-five years ago you said, "Your life is a book!" Those words got planted in my soul. Thank you for the countless hours of editing and re-editing. You are brilliant and loved. To my agent Frank Breeden for immediately believing in this project. Melanie Friebel and Bobbie Metevier for your time and talent. To all the pre-readers and cherished friends who challenged and pushed me to do and be better; Sandy, Jill, Cindy, Terri, Melissa, Marie, Karie, Lenny, Tracy, Karin, Stacey Jo, Laura, Kathy, Karen, Laura, Klavdja, Tonda and Diane. To the Culture Club: Laurens, Donna and Amy, for the enormous amount of inspiration, pasta and laughter. To Paul Miller for helping many of these stories come to life. To Phil and Kathy Cooke for being such bright lights. To my families: The Rinks and The Hrovats (both in the United States and Slovenia) for your unwavering patience and love. To my siblings for allowing me share your stories too. To Jim: your love for our son is one of the most comforting and beautiful things I have ever experienced. Thank you for being our rock. And to James, whose life gave me life. Bobby loves you.

"One meets his destiny often in the road he takes to avoid it."
~ *French Proverb* ~

Preface

Destiny

I thrashed around in my bed like a fish on cement gasping for air. It was a bitter cold December morning, just four days before Christmas, and I was drowning in pain. The tears fell out of my eyes like a hard spring rain, soaking the pillow that I grasped for strength. "I knew it! I knew it! I just knew it!" I screamed, as I pounded my fist on the bed. "Why, why, why didn't I listen to my gut?" Now, there was no turning back. There would be no do-over. It was all going to happen just like I always knew it would.

I would give birth to a special needs child.

I know it sounds crazy. It still sounds crazy to me some days. But this is why I will never argue with the people on TV who swear they have been abducted by aliens. It is their truth.

This was mine.

I'm not sure how I knew it. But I knew it like you know when you're hungry, or tired. Like how you know what day it is. And the knowing was there from the very beginning. From my very first thoughts about having kids. It was the reason why I insisted my husband Jim and I see a geneticist before I went off the pill at thirty-five. It was why I put off trying to get pregnant for nearly twenty years. And it was absolutely why I was secretly relieved after each of my two miscarriages. The loss of a baby wasn't nearly as important as my need to keep the perception of my perfect life intact. I breathed a huge sigh of relief that I had narrowly escaped my fate.

Escaping and hiding had become a way of life for me. I was a skilled master of disguise, like a chameleon, morphing into whomever people wanted or needed me to be. Or whatever would make me look and feel the best. Lying in that bed, at forty years old, was a woman who had no clue who her true self even was. That girl went missing from a crib on Stanley Avenue.

5193 Stanley Avenue

I grew up in the white house with the four porch pillars on Stanley Avenue in Maple Heights, Ohio, a suburb of Cleveland. At the time, it was an immigrant middle class suburban neighborhood, with large oak trees and Chevys and babushkas. From the outside, our family looked perfect. But inside our 1000-square-foot house were six kids, one bathroom and my mother's unlimited supply of valium, and we were nothing but lost.

I am the daughter of Ludwig Hrovat, entertainer and life-of-the-party alcoholic father, which is sometimes worse than the angry abusive kind. You know you are supposed to feel bad when you get physically hit. Emotional wounds are harder to justify. My father worked three jobs and ruled the house even though he was never home. My mother, Lillian, was an outwardly strong and funny, but inwardly sad and depressed, codependent. She loved her husband and her kids and her Pall Malls, but not necessarily in that order. My dad called me the "caboose": the last in line of six kids, all addicts.

There are sixteen years between my oldest brother and myself, so their lives and stories were my teachers. I watched and feared Lud Jr.'s addiction to heroin, Larry's transformation from college football hero and alcoholic to evangelist, and Lenny's journey from being addicted to prescription pills to becoming a drug and alcohol counselor. I watched my sister Kathy spend money she didn't have

The Hrovat Siblings, circa 1997

to get high by gambling, and my sister Karie choose and be left by men that looked and acted just like my dad, or not. Someone once asked my husband Jim, "If Lynn comes from a family of addicts, what is her addiction?" He answered confidently, "Music! And don't let her fool you — it's more powerful than heroin!"

But more on that later.

My mother became the circus master, the ringleader, and her sole purpose in life was to "keep the dysfunction functioning" until she was too tired to keep all the plates in the air. She was fifty-six, I was seventeen, and it was cancer. She found a lump and everything came crashing down. Three months and eight days later she was gone, leaving behind an emptiness that would fill me for the next twenty-five years. And with her last breath, she took my barely breathing sense of self with her.

I went away to college at a state school, just a few hours from my home. I thought using alcohol would take away my pain. It didn't. Then, after a visit to see my evangelist brother, I became a born again Christian and transferred to a strict Christian college with the hope that Jesus would take away the ache in my heart. He didn't. One year later, I married a man for all the wrong reasons with the belief that he would rescue me. He tried for twenty-five years, but couldn't.

There was only one person who could save me.

I'm a dreamer, not just while awake, but while I sleep. I've had several reoccurring dreams for as long as I can remember. One of

3

them is that I'm at a party and everyone is warning me not to stand too close to the wall or a snake will get on my head. A snake? I hate snakes. "What the hell am I doing at a party that would even allow snakes?" I am careful, but somehow I end up against the wall and a huge python sits on my head. I run around begging everyone to please take the snake off my head, screaming and crying, "Please, please help me!" But they can't hear me. No one can hear me. Eventually, extremely exhausted, I sit down in a corner, the weight of the snake pushing me to the floor and its long body wrapping around my neck. With no other options, I slowly reach up to try to remove the snake myself, and just as my fingers touch its body, it turns to dust in my hand.

I had my first counseling session at twenty-three and became a sort of self-help junkie. I'd been in and out of therapy consistently. I wept on many couches. I could quote the Serenity Prayer. But it wouldn't be until years after my son James was born with Down syndrome, that I would even begin to understand the truth—the truth that, just like my father, I became an entertainer and hid from myself and others behind the sweet sounds of the accordion. And, just like my mother, I became a raging codependent. But I didn't even know what that word meant, really, until I stopped being it one day and felt the difference.

A friend said to me once, "Lynn, if you knew you were going to have a special needs child, then why did you try to get pregnant for the third time?" Honestly, after two miscarriages, I just assumed it wouldn't last. I hoped it wouldn't last. And the failed attempt would at least temporarily satisfy Jim's desire to be a dad and my need to appear to do the next right thing.

I'd like to make a few things clear before we go on. First, this is my story, and it is true. From my perspective. As I was doing research for this book I realized that each person remembers the story differently. There are as many versions of the event as there are people who experienced it. And each memory is shaped by that person's ability or inability to cope with the circumstances at the time. Secondly, a lot of things happened in the white space, in the margins, and in between the lines, which I don't feel are relevant to the telling of this particular journey. As in life, the hard part is knowing what to leave out. And third, this is in fact an ongoing journey. Jim and I are still trying to figure out who we are as a couple and who we are as parents of a special needs child. And even though our lives have been intertwined for thirty years (and will continue to be because of the bond we share with James), we are not always on the same page when it comes to our beliefs in potty training, the remote control, and God.

Oh, and one last thing. I hate Down syndrome. Most days I would give anything to not have a child with this syndrome or any other syndrome. One time an organization asked me to write an article explaining in five hundred words or less, the upside of Down syndrome. My first response was, "Is there one?"

But then, when James makes his way up onto my lap and in his awkward tongue says "Hi Bobby" (I am Bobby instead of mommy), I smile and realize how thankful I am for this obvious necessary gift.

James is in fact a gift, not because of what he has, but because of what he has given me. The ability to stop. Down syndrome was the only thing that could stop me from running from the one thing I could never get away from.

And in the early morning hours, when Fido (my slightly psychotic, pain-in-the-ass, yet extremely loyal cocker spaniel) and I are the only ones awake, and the sky is just turning from black to blue, I still wonder about the fine gray lines of it all. How did I know this was all going to happen? What was that? Did God know and plan this all along? Does He (or She because I believe God is Spirit and not a physical being with gender) let bad things happen? Did my higher power know that this was the only way I would eventually learn to listen to my gut and get unstuck? Or, did my intense focus on not wanting it and having it in the frontal lobe of my brain all those years, actually summon the universe to bring it to me? Then, I take a deep breath, sip my Diet Pepsi, eat another Oreo, watch Fido sniff for crumbs and conclude it doesn't matter. It just doesn't matter.

In the end (and in the beginning) I try to not get hung up on that part of the story. James is here, and what happened to me because of his arrival, before his arrival and after his arrival, is and will always be my truth. I believe that everything happens for a reason, but the goodness and beauty of it does not unfold until you have the courage and desire to see it.

People sometimes use the words destiny and fate interchangeably. But, they are actually quite different. Webster's Dictionary defines fate as the "Unfavorable outcome of predetermined events" and destiny as "Past events that have already worked themselves out, achieving an outcome that is directly related to itself." If this is true, then according to Webster, what I ran from was my fate—what I finally accepted was my destiny. And in that acceptance I would come to know that God and my gut are one in the same, and I love them both.

> *"When you are sorrowful look again in your heart, and you
> shall see that in truth you are weeping for that which
> has been your delight."*
> ~ *Khalil Gibran* ~

1.

THE CLOSET

It was cold that night, especially for California. Forty-three and dreary, which described me as well. I sat in the hot tub and stared up at the stars peeking in and out from behind the moving clouds. Raindrops landed on my cheeks. They became one with my tears and slowly made their way into my ears, settling there, leaving wide black mascara tracks behind. "This fucking sucks," I mumbled.

I had just returned to our rental house in Venice Beach, after attending the 51st Annual Grammy Awards in Los Angeles. And I kept repeating out loud over and over, as if hearing myself say it would somehow help ease the pain, "Well...it was just an honor to have been nominated...for the fifth time!" Yes, I am a five-time Grammy loser, or winner I suppose, depending on whether your glass is half empty or half full. But I've had enough therapy now to accept the fact that I am officially the Susan Lucci of Polka.

But do you want to know the truth? Do you want to know what I was really feeling? It wasn't enough to just be nominated. It was never enough. I hated having to smile and say those words with every interview that followed the loss. I wanted to say what I truly felt, that I was sad and tired and I wanted to win the damn trophy. I wanted to say that I had spent months and thousands of dollars to win the damn trophy! That I needed to win the damn trophy so that my career might have a fighting chance. I was bitter and angry because I am obviously not a good loser. But I also know that I would not have been a good winner. And quite possibly I didn't deserve to win. Even though I knew we always had one of the most creative and innovative sounding albums in the category, my heart was not right. My motivation was completely out of whack and I know I wouldn't have been able to handle a win. My mental state, my marriage, my career would not have survived. So I am extremely grateful for what I believe is God's grace and mercy and protection, but I still can't help but wonder if it would have been too much to ask to win just ONE of the five damn trophies?

> We pray for things that we think will fulfill
> us and make us happy. What we get are
> opportunities for internal change so we can
> choose to be happy.

I positioned my legs just right so that the jets could massage my blistered feet (you'd think after five times down the red carpet I'd learn to buy comfortable shoes) and I thought, "Now what?" I had done this for almost eight years. Lose the Grammy. Figure out how to pay my American Express bill. Go back into studio. Release a new recording in the spring. Struggle to get enough gigs to survive the summer. Campaign for Grammy in the fall. Lose Grammy. Smile through the pain. Repeat. But this time the thought of going back into the studio didn't feel right. Creatively I had nothing left. I had nothing new to offer. I had disguised polka and myself everyway I knew how. I needed something different.

And that's when I heard it.

A voice.

I don't usually go around hearing voices or seeing things that aren't there, and I don't consider myself to be one of *those* people. I do consider myself a new believer in the Law of Attraction and "Oprah's Super Soul Sunday", an old believer of God and Jesus and a forever believer in Santa Claus. Regardless, it wasn't a James Earl Jones-ish kind of voice. It wasn't even external. It came up from within. And it was small and faint and caring. It was the voice we all have inside of us that longs to guide and direct us, but we usually have to be at our wit's end and out of options before we'll listen.

Which I was. So I did.

What it said was very simple, "Lynn. It's time to stop."

I tried to ignore it at first, moving so the jets could attack my lower back, but then I heard it again, this time a bit louder and more emphatic, like the voice of my mother when I had worn her down to her last nerve, caring yet stern, "Kid, it's time to stop!" My therapist Diane had suggested this option several months ago, but it SO didn't work for me. During one particularly emotional session I found myself curled up in a ball on her floor. She asked me, "Lynn what would happen if you stopped?"

"Stopped what?" I asked, pretending not to know what she was getting at.

"Stopped everything. Stopped hiding. Stopped lying. Stopped running. Stopped performing." She finally landed on one I could justify.

"Oh my God, I could never stop performing. Everything would fall apart."

Then she said, "Lynn, you are laying on my floor completely covered in snot. I'm thinking everything already is apart."

She was right. But stopping meant giving up, letting go and losing. I don't lose. But now, with the sting of a fifth loss laying on me like bad sunburn, stopping seemed like a better idea than it ever had before. I was tired.

For almost twenty years I had traveled the country trying to convince anyone who would listen that polka music was cool and hip. It wasn't necessarily my fault; I really didn't have a choice. It was in my blood. Something I couldn't control, like being born into a circus family or a Jehovah's Witness. My mother used to make me hide behind the wingback chair in the living room when they would knock on our front door. When I see them now, walking down the street in their black and white outfits, kids in tow, I wonder about those kids. If they understand what they are doing and more importantly, do they want to do it? But they don't have a choice yet. And early on, neither did I. This was the home and the culture that I was born into. We were surrounded by ethnicity. Steeped in it, like the mafia—minus the killing parts. There may not have been any dead bodies lying around, but plenty of things got snuffed out.

Žužemberk, Slovenia

My grandparents emigrated from the northernmost republic of the former Yugoslavia, Slovenia, which is now a country about the size of New Jersey that borders Italy, Austria and Croatia.

On one side you have the Alps and on the other the Adriatic Sea. And in the middle, rolling hills covered in family-owned vineyards. As you drive the country roads you see village after village, and in the center of each, a Catholic church on the highest hilltop. The people are kind and honest and rich with customs and traditions, which include folk music played primarily on accordions.

The Slovenian immigrants tried their best to recreate their homeland on the streets of Maple Heights. St. Wenceslas Church sat in the center of our village, but what grounded us, what grounded them, was The Slovenian National Home at the end of Stanley Avenue.

"The Nash" as we called it, was built in 1937 and was a cross between an English pub and a German dance hall. In early records of the construction process it says, "They decided to place the joists on 12-inch centers rather than 16-inch as per the plans. They knew the foot-stomping Slovene polkas required a stronger dancing platform than the plans originally offered." This pretty much sums up the Slovenian immigrants.

They survived a transatlantic crossing, many on freight boats. They faced ridicule and were taken advantage of because they didn't speak the language. They weathered the Great Depression. And through it all they didn't lose their pioneer spirit or their love for dancing and music.

The Slovenian National Home in Maple Heights, circa 1974

The Nash was my second home. I made the walk hundreds of times from my house, past the Stepaniks and Lorinces, around the bend in front of the Zupancics and Hocevars to the corner of Stanley and Raymond. It was a split-

Ludwig Hrovat, age 11

level blond brick building with two large orange metal doors at the front. The doors were heavy and loud and I used to have to use my whole body to open them. Once inside, the smell of cigarettes and floor polish and klobasi (Slovenian smoked sausage) would welcome me. Walking through those doors always felt safer than walking into my own house. Weddings and anniversary parties and baby showers were all held at The Nash. And if you

13

booked your wedding reception there in the sixties, you got the house band—The Lud Hrovat Orchestra. I'd sit on the edge of the two-foot-high stage and watch my daddy perform. The people would waltz by and smile at him, then he would look down at me, and with a glance give the command. It was my job to refill his glass of scotch.

My dad picked up the accordion when he was about eleven. When he returned from the Navy at age nineteen, he started his

band. And up until the day when he could no longer physically pick up his box, he entertained any chance he got. He was not the best accordion player, or the best singer, but he could entertain like no one else. People were drawn to him and to his spirit and this made him the life of the party. Everyone loved Lud. Everyone that is, at the party. But when the music stopped, and the last guest stumbled home, underneath

Lud's Tavern, circa 1969

that fun-loving exterior was a hardworking, stubborn, unpredictable alcoholic. He was a person you could love and hate in the same second. He would give you the shirt off his back, and then he'd turn around and tell you that you looked like shit in it.

My mother did the best she could raising us, with a husband who

was never home. My dad spent every waking hour at his bar, Lud's Tavern, just a mile from our house. Our home became an extension to the tavern, the back screen door flimsy from constant use of people coming and going. We had an open bar policy and we had some of the

First Communion Party, 1972

best parties.

~

The lace on my First Holy Communion dress scratched my thin boney legs as I tugged on my white knee-high socks and bounced into the living room. The room was full of family members and neighbors, casually chatting and sipping their Tom Collinses and Schlitz beers. But I was bored. I had already opened a mound of cards with crosses and prayers on them and handed over a ton of cash to my mom. I had cut the large sheet cake with my silver engraved cake knife that read, "Congratulations LynnMarie." There was only one thing that left to do. Beg my dad to get out his accordion.

And when he did, in an instant, everything changed. People got happy. He got happy. It was as if someone rolled back the roof and dumped in a load of joy. Everyone started laughing and dancing and drinking more. I twirled and waltzed and sang "Oj Marička Pegla" and "I've Been Working on the Railroad". My sister Kathy brought in a second pitcher of Grasshoppers to drink and Auntie Rosie refilled the Tupperware tray with olives and pickles. In between songs, my dad would do a shot and a beer with Uncle Gas and light another cigarette that would burn in the ashtray while he played the next song. Music always made everything better.

This party was no different than the hundreds before, but something happened to me that day, something clicked inside. As I watched my dad play, I understood more than just the words to the Slovenian folk songs he was singing. That day, at only seven years old, I recognized the power of music to change people's spirits. The power to change *my* spirit. And I knew that's what I wanted to do.

Then, I looked around that room and realized that every eye was on my father, and I thought, "If I played, well then even *he* would have to notice me."

For the next three years, I begged my parents for an accordion. (That could be the least written sentence in the English language.) Finally, when I was eleven, my dad walked in the back door one random Friday afternoon carrying a borrowed 1940's Lubas diatonic button accordion. It was beat up and worn in, but I didn't care. I finally had my hands on the tool that would get me into my father's heart.

A cigarette with a long ash dangled from his mouth as he pulled the box out of the case. He placed the thick embroidered straps over each of my shoulders and secured them in the back with one of his old black ties. I felt the straps tighten and then release slightly as the weight of the box fell onto me. I'll never forget the look in his eyes that day. He seemed so proud, even though I couldn't really play. I knew I had his attention. I thought that meant I had his love and acceptance too.

It wouldn't be until I was in my forties, and he was close to death, that I would finally understand that playing the accordion wasn't going to do it. That no matter how many trophies I won or songs I wrote or Grammys I had lost – what I was longing for, craving to receive from him, was something he was simply incapable of giving.

Even so, from the moment I strapped it on, I never wanted to play anything else. The accordion became my first love, my escape, my shield, my drug, my partner in crime, for better or worse, for richer or poorer (mostly poorer) 'til death do us part.

~

I sat in that hot tub for hours. The rain had stopped and the skin on my fingertips had shriveled like raisins. I thought about just staying there. Putting the cover back on over top of me. Even though 'Death by Jacuzzi' would have made a great newspaper headline, my ego would not have been satisfied. I also worried no one would look for me.

I stood up. It was cold. I wrapped myself in a beach towel and thought of all the times I wrapped James in a towel like a burrito after giving him a bath, wanting him to feel warm and safe. I pulled my towel tighter.

The house was quiet. One of my best friends, KC (which stands for Kathy from Canada, so we wouldn't get her and my sister Kathy confused) was asleep on the large sectional couch in the living room. Lanyards for red carpet access and torn ticket stubs and my nomination medal, instead of a trophy, sat on the countertop. I tiptoed to my room, leaving drops of water behind, as if I was shedding. I slid into bed. Jim was asleep and yet I could still feel his frustration. Not because I lost, but because I was incapable of sharing my pain with him.

I stared at the ceiling fan, watching it go round and round and round, and I made the half-hearted decision to stop performing and get off the road. I wanted it to be whole-hearted, but I was scared and exhausted and my heart was in pieces and I had no idea how to pick them up. I had no plan or vision for what to do next, but I knew stopping would change everything. I recalled a quote I had seen on a plaque in Diane's office that read, "Insanity is doing the same thing over and over expecting different results." There was a part of me that knew I had been acting insane for years. It's easy to do in order to avoid your pain. But the voice inside me had gotten through just enough that night and got me thinking about change.

I hate change. It hurts. It's like going to the dentist to get teeth pulled to make room for new ones. I didn't know it then, but what I was about to do was not just change, but make room for growth. For the first time in years I was letting life in, instead of keeping it out. I think I would have enjoyed it more if there had been laughing gas involved.

> Space creates opportunity. When we stop doing something, we allow space to enter. Maybe that space gets filled with a new job or a new relationship. For me that space carried the sound of my own voice.

In therapy I would learn about the *Stages of Change*. First there is pre-contemplation, where the thought of change never even enters your brain. Then contemplation, when you start to have these fleeting moments about how what you're doing isn't working and maybe, just maybe making a change would be a good thing. But this stage can last anywhere from a moment — to an entire lifetime. And this was the stage I was at. Not fully committed but yet knowing I needed to do something. The remaining stages, determination, action and maintenance would still be many tears and years away.

I returned home from the Grammys and, as I unpacked my suitcase, I found myself mumbling and alternating between, "I can't believe I lost again," to "It was an honor just to be nominated," to "Lynn, you have to stop," as I moved performance clothes to the back of the closet. And with every hanger I picked up and every stage shirt I put away, I felt like I was letting go bit by bit of what I had spent my whole life trying to achieve. I was so afraid my career was ending in that closet. I was so afraid *I* was ending in that closet. And I was even more afraid that being home and not on the road would force me to spend time with my son.

James was now two and a half and I knew on one level I had missed all of it up to that point. All of it. I had been physically present for his birth, his first trip to the beach, his first word, and his ear tube surgery. But I was emotionally checked out. I got only as close as I needed too. And with every day, week, and month that passed, I knew I was not being a great mother. I knew leaving him on the floor of his room for hours while I finished one more email or made one more phone call was not the right thing to do. Motherhood was hard for me. Still is actually. Some people, like my sister Karie, wear motherhood like a second skin. Mine felt like a rash.

I picked up my German dirndl top. I had purchased it in a small shop in Austria while on tour in 2007. I wore it to play the Oktoberfests in Mt. Angel, Oregon, and Puyallup, Washington. Some of the best gigs ever. Thousands of drunken kids dancing to my band playing "Mama's Got a Squeeze Box" by The Who, disguised as a polka. And me on stage disguised as a happy, full of life entertainer. I reluctantly pushed it to the back of the closet. And then I glanced out the window.

The window in our closet overlooks our driveway. And when I looked down, I tried to imagine myself two or three years down the road, Kindergarten time, walking James to the end of the drive to wait for the school bus. I thought fondly for a moment of my time as a child waiting for the school bus at the end of our driveway on Stanley Avenue. But when I looked up, what I saw coming down the street to get James was not the regular school bus.

It was the short bus.

The vision of that bus, half the size as the real school bus, stopped in front of my house brought me to my knees. "I can't do this!" I screamed. "I can NOT do this!" The anger and fear reared up inside me like untamable monsters. There was not one part of me that thought I had what it would take to handle life with James nor did I want to. "I don't want this, God! And I just can't wrap my head around the fact that I have a special needs child!"

In the silence that followed the screams, the voice deep in my gut was clear.

"Lynn, I'm not asking you to wrap your head around it; I'm asking you to wrap your heart around it."

I collapsed into a pile of dirty laundry in pseudo-surrender. I blew my nose in a sock. This was not surrender in its glorious form, like an alter call with beautiful organ music playing and light streaming through a stained glass window. It was surrender mixed in with exhaustion and fear and surrounded by dirty underwear.

Which I personally think God loves. It doesn't get more real than dirty underwear. And on that closet floor, I let go just enough to let a sliver of light seep into the cracks of my broken heart.

I had known my whole life that James was coming. And I logically knew Down syndrome was something I couldn't physically fix. I recalled Diane's words to me, just before I left for the Grammys: "Lynn, sometimes in life you get a steel wall.

It comes in, it slams down hard, and it becomes part of your being from that point on—and there's nothing you can do about it! You can't go around it. You can't go through it. You can't fix it."

Apparently she didn't understand that I was the world's greatest codependent and I fix everyone and everything and desperately need to in order to have any amount of self-worth. But in that closet that day, I somehow understood that I was powerless over this one. I got it. I get it. I got it.

I can't fix it.

But, I had no idea how to love it.

> *"It sounds corny, but I've promised my inner child that never
> again will I ever abandon myself for anything or anyone."*
> ~ *Wynonna Judd* ~

2.

SUNDAYS

As I drove the coastal highway that winds from La Jolla to Pacific Beach in San Diego one Sunday afternoon, the beauty alone should have been breathtaking; instead all I could think of was taking my own breath away. "If I just turn the wheel hard enough, I will plummet off this rocky cliff into the ocean and it will look like an accident."

That was the first time I contemplated suicide.

At only twenty-four, this should have been the time of my life. Jim and I were going on three years of marriage; we were living in paradise and had our whole lives in front of us. And yet, nothing felt right. I had just returned from a trip to Slovenia with my father where I had met my relatives for the first time and played my accordion and partied and drank homemade whiskey, Slivovica. All no-nos according to the born again Christians I was living with and around. I came home and told Jim, "Look, I don't know what I think about God, and I don't know what I believe about marriage. The only thing I do know is that I want to play the accordion." He was angry and scared and silent. When I became a born again Christian I made the decision to quit playing. Jim and I met and were married just a year later, and the accordion was moved to the back of every closet of every apartment we lived in. Now it was out in the family room and in my life like an ex-lover. We both felt stuck. I felt stuck in a job I hated, working for a television evangelist. Stuck in a marriage that didn't feel right. Stuck in a religion I believed had lied to me.

Somehow, I pulled off that winding road and into a parking lot to compose myself. I was sobbing uncontrollably and when I looked up, I was staring at a Catholic church. How ironic. This was the closest I'd been to a Catholic church since I had become a born again Christian six years earlier.

I knew enough to know what I was looking for wasn't in the sanctuary. I needed a body, not a symbol. I thought back to the rectory at St. Wenceslas Church. "There's always someone in the rectory," I remembered. So I knocked on the door. I couldn't speak, yet somehow through my tears (and I'm guessing the presence of running mascara) the receptionist understood that I needed help and welcomed me in. She took me to an unoccupied office. I watched her discreetly pick up the letter opener from the desk and take it with her as she left. A few minutes later she came back in and picked up the phone on the desk and handed it to me. "It's one of our church counselors, Bob, who would like to speak with you," she said and left the room.

I heard the voice on the other end of the phone, "Hey Lynn, my name is Bob and I'm going to help you. Can you come to my office tomorrow at 3 p.m.?"

"Yes." I replied.

"Okay," he said. "And what are you going to do between now and then?" I didn't quite understand what he was wanting to know.

"Um, I'm gonna go home?" I said, hoping that was the response he was looking for.

"Okay, but you're not gonna hurt yourself between now and tomorrow at 3 p.m., are you? I need you to promise me that you're going to come to my office tomorrow."

I assured him I'd be there.

I wasn't sure what I thought about therapy. I knew about it. Had heard about it. Growing up with a house full of addicts I knew that people went occasionally. But those were sick people. Really sick people. People, who, like my brother Lud, had tried to commit suicide.

The next day I walked into Bob's office, tucked away in a strip mall off of Rancho Penasquitos Boulevard. I liked him immediately and when I shook his hand I didn't want to let go. His office was small but comfortable with a micro-suede brown love seat, a wooden chair, a single side table with a lamp and the obligatory box of Kleenex. Which I used. A lot.

Bob was obviously Catholic, since I found him at the Catholic church. And although I wasn't sure about his belief in the Eucharist as more than a symbol, it was comforting to have someone from my past nearby. I didn't know Bob when I was little, but he knew me. He had lived in a house just like mine. With crosses on the walls and palms over the doorways and statues of the Mother Mary. I promised myself that I would take the good he had to offer and filter out the stuff that my born again Christian beliefs didn't agree with.

Bob let me talk for the entire hour. Then he said he really thought what I was going through might have something to do with the way I was raised. He asked me to take the next week and write down everything traumatic and anything life-changing that I could think of that had happened in my childhood.

I stopped him. "Oh no, no you don't. I'm not going to be one of those people who blame their parents for why they are so screwed up."

He calmly said,

"Learning about your past and who your parents were is not about blame. It's about understanding."

For the next week I worked on a time line. I called my siblings and asked about accidents and jail stays and wedding dates. When I finished I was shocked to discover that my family had something traumatic happen every year for almost ten years straight. How could my mother survive this? For the first time I began to look at the story of my life. Not just my Slovenian roots, but my family's story. Who my parents were, who their parents were, what they taught me that I accepted as truth and why. As I wrote, I remembered more than just events. I remembered smells and sounds and fear. I showed up the next week with multiple pages of white, lined paper, filled to the margins.

~

I was five years old when I stood at the top of the converted attic staircase listening, terrified of what might await me below. All I could hear was static. Static and strange men's voices echoed through the house. Voices from the police radio that sat on the kitchen counter. My mom had a friend who worked for the Maple Heights Police Department, and she somehow convinced him to give her one. I overheard Auntie Olga, my dad's sister, ask her once why she needed a police radio. "I just like to know what's going on in the city," she said. What she meant was that she liked to know what was going on in her own house. With a police radio, she could keep track of her kids. She would know when one of them was arrested or in a car accident or missing.

When I reached the bottom of the steps my clothes were laid out on the back of the high-back barstool that sat at the counter. My mom helped me get dressed; a maroon and gray plaid jumper that landed just above the knee, a white blouse and a grey cardigan sweater. This would be my daily uniform for the next eight years.

Outside the rain was pounding on the window awnings as my mom pushed the over-the-shoe galoshes onto my saddle shoes, buttoned up my floral raincoat, opened my umbrella, and sent me out to wait for the school bus at the end of our driveway. The bus stop had been at the end of our driveway since my brother Lud started at St. Wenceslas over ten years earlier. A white, curved stone bench, not any bigger than room for two small kids to sit on, sat at the corner where the driveway met the sidewalk. We grew up on that bench. So much life happens in the ten minutes you spend at a school bus stop.

My childhood friend Luddy Bergman (Little Luddy) and I sat on the bench in the pouring rain. My feet were cold. It was the first week of Kindergarten. Then Little Luddy asked the obvious question, but one that, even at five, I knew he shouldn't ask: "Hey, why can't we stand on your front porch out of the rain and wait for the school bus?"

Before I could stop it, "No" came barreling up from inside and out my lips. I felt fear replace the cold in my toes. I realized that something was different about my dad, and that while he slept, just on the other side of that porch wall, no matter if it meant I would be soaking wet and shivering, I shouldn't wake him.

When I got off the bus that afternoon the rain had stopped and the sun had dried the grass and it needed mowing. My brother Lenny got it done just in time before my dad got home from the bar. My dad would come home from the bar every afternoon at 3:15 to change his worn-in white work shirt for a crisp new one. I sat on the front porch and watched our red Lincoln Continental pull in the driveway. My dad got out, threw his half-smoked Lark cigarette onto the pavement, and put it out with his wingtip shoe. He stood there, for what seemed like hours, staring at the front lawn. Finally, in a tone so full of anger it was as if his breath alone would kill the red and white petunias at his feet, he said, "Who cut the grass?"

Lenny made his way from the side yard. His pre-teen blond hair swooped down covering his left eye and his shoulders slumped over as if he was trying to disappear. You see, this was a trick question. If by chance my dad was happy that the grass was cut, well, then you wanted the recognition. But what if he wasn't? Finally, lifting his eyes to meet my father's Lenny said, "I cut it." There was another long pause. I wanted to run but was too afraid to move. My father slammed the car door.

"God dammit—you cut it with the lines going the wrong way!"

At this point in his life my father was drinking a case of beer and a fifth of whiskey a day, along with opening up his fourth pack of cigarettes. He had no idea what he was doing to his kids, to his wife and to himself. He had no idea that his children lived in fear of him. That we walked on our tiptoes around him and that his drinking made us unsure of everything. The only thing we were completely sure of was that we didn't matter. The only thing that mattered was that we played our part and took care of the alcoholic. As Diane would say, "You were merely playing parts in the Lud movie."

Communication in our house was pared down to necessity. And the words "I love you" were never said. Never. We never hugged or kissed each other. Outward expression of any kind, except disapproval, was frowned upon. And I'm sure this was not uncommon behavior for immigrant families in the seventies. It was a different era. So the only time I can recall hugging my parents was during the Sign of Peace at Sunday mass. And it always felt awkward.

Since we were Catholic that meant that we went to church on Sunday unless we were dying, and even then, maybe we should go in case it was our last chance to take communion. However, my father usually only went to church on Easter and Christmas and Ash Wednesday; for the occasions when you had to go to show the neighbors that you were doing all the right things. Especially Ash Wednesday because then there was proof—the ashes on your forehead were a symbol of repentance and sorrow and commitment to the Gospels. But when you're standing in front of the priest, he doesn't ask if you are feeling any of these things when he makes the sign of the cross on your forehead. Anyone can get ashes.

There was that rare occasion when my dad would go to mass on any old Sunday. Maybe he had had a particularly bad Saturday night and woke with a heavy heart. Or maybe he never went to bed? I don't know. But one time my dad went with me to the 10:30 a.m. contemporary mass in the St. Wenceslas Grade School gym. I liked going to this service because they had acoustic guitars and singers and Father Joe.

Father Joe was the cool priest; he gave short sermons, told jokes and stopped by the house occasionally for a glass of wine. His presence in our home was as if royalty had arrived. The best silver came out, the good wine was poured (from the back of the liquor cabinet), and people acted differently. I never understood this. But the air would get thin, like everyone was holding their breath, so as not to let out any secrets.

During the mass that Sunday when Father Joe said, "Let's offer up the Sign of Peace," my dad hugged me, awkwardly, and that's when I smelled it. Beer. Whiskey. Cigarettes.

Why was I smelling this on Sunday morning at church? I mean, I smell it a lot at home, at parties, at the bar, but now in church? It just didn't seem right.

My dad tried to hold my hand as we walked to the car but I pulled away. I remember feeling that something was different about my dad compared to the other dads in that parking lot. I was always so proud of being able to say, "My dad owns Lud's Tavern on Libby

Road." But that day, as we drove past it on the way home, I turned my head and sunk in the front seat.

Once home, the smells on my father blended in with the chaos of a typical Hrovat Sunday. The house was packed with friends and family. Loud angry conversations filled the air along with the thick layer of cigarette smoke. Music, combined with AM radio static, came out of the six-foot-long stereo console system we had in the living room. Listening to Tony Petkovsek's Polka Radio show was almost as important as going to mass. I was handed a klobasi wrapped in a piece of Auntie Olga's homemade bread.

And I waited.

I was sure one of the adults was going to say something about my father being drunk. Surely someone was going to yell at him or make him go to bed? But nobody said anything.

Ever.

And with every bite of sausage, I tried to swallow the confusing thoughts that had surfaced that morning. And then they arrived. The mean voices. It's the first time I remember being aware of my own thoughts. "Lynn, maybe you're wrong? Look around you, everything is okay. Your dad is happy. No one else seems concerned. Are you sure you smelled something? I bet you didn't smell anything. You must be wrong. You ARE wrong."

~

Bob had tears in his eyes when we finished reading. He put the papers down and looked at me and said, "Lynn, I'm so sorry. I'm so sorry you had to go through all this."

I became defensive, which surprised me. I tried to tell him that I had good parents and a good childhood and I wasn't physically abused, or raped, or homeless. There was nothing earth-shattering on those pages. Just parties and car accidents and deaths and memories. "This is just the kind of stuff that happens in big families," I said, trying to convince both him and myself.

And then he said something I would never forget:

> "It's not the stuff that happened to that little girl that worries me. It's what happened to that little girl in the midst of the stuff."

I started crying. The deepest tears. Old tears. Ones that I swore would never see the light of day. And I cried for what felt like weeks. Something was happening at a level deeper than anything I'd ever experienced. He was right. It wasn't about blame. It was about understanding. It was the first time I was looking at me. Who I was, what I thought, what I believed. And how my childhood and the environment I was raised in shaped me.

It didn't take long for me to see what happened to the little girl; she became a—and this is my least favorite word in the English language—codependent. It's like fingers on a chalkboard. I hate it because it gets thrown around a lot, over used and misused, which means people are becoming numb to it. Like when people thank God on award shows. Nobody cares because it's expected now to thank God, so it means less and less for those who truly are thankful to God.

There are many definitions of codependency, as many as there are people who suffer from the disease. But when I read *Codependent No More* by Melody Beattie, I knew she was talking about me.

> "...*codependency involves a habitual system of thinking, feeling, and behaving toward ourselves and others that can cause us pain. Codependent behaviors or habits are self-destructive. We frequently react to people who are destroying themselves; we react by learning to destroy ourselves. These habits can lead us into, or keep us in, destructive relationships, relationships that don't work. These behaviors can sabotage relationships that may otherwise have worked. These behaviors can prevent us from finding peace and happiness with the most important person in our lives—ourselves. These behaviors belong to the only person each of us can control—the only person we can change—ourselves.*" (p. 37)

29

After a couple of sessions with Bob, I began to understand what it meant to be a codependent. For me, it meant I thought if I could find a way to be cute enough, or quiet enough, or play the accordion just right, then maybe my dad wouldn't drink. I truly thought I had this kind of power. And later in life, when I had given up on the hope that my dad would ever quit drinking, I focused my codependency on anything and anyone I could get my hands on: Jim, jobs, music, producers, dogs and James. I was so wounded internally, so full of shame, that I desperately needed an external inflow of things and people to make me feel better. To give me any amount of self-worth.

I also learned about not having the freedom to have my own thoughts, my own desires and ultimately my own voice. In our house what we needed as kids didn't matter, what we thought didn't matter. All that mattered was we played our parts and took care of the alcoholic.

Bob modeled my therapy after the work of John Bradshaw and his book *Homecoming*. He said the little girl in me didn't get some of her basic needs met, and she was still in there crying out, just now in a twenty-six-year-old body. Part of it sounded goofy and wimpy, but I was hurting and I wanted the pain to stop, so I went with it.

Being a therapy junkie is kind of like being a sugar addict. Some people get it, and some people don't. Some people love Krispy Kreme donuts when the HOT NOW light is on and some people can drive by without even noticing it. (How is that possible by the way?) So terms like codependency, dysfunction and inner child either ring true for you, or you will drive right by. Until maybe the day comes when your insides are craving answers and you are willing to stop and indulge.

Week after week, I mentally went back and talked to that little girl sitting at that kitchen table, holding her klobasi, Slovenian folk songs playing in the background as the mean voices went on and on in her head.

And this is what I told her.

"You are not wrong! You are absolutely right! What you smelled on your father was booze, and lots of it, because he is an alcoholic. And you are not crazy. All the adults in this house are ignoring it because they can't even begin to deal with that reality or their own pain. Making you feel crazy is easier. What you don't know as a little girl is that you can never please an alcoholic. They will always want something better, something different, something more. You cannot fill the hole they have inside, the reason they drink in the first place. They will always want the lines on the grass to go the other way."

The work I committed to doing with Bob was hard. But I loved the process. I loved finding the truth in the past and how it was affecting me in the present. But it would take another twenty years, lots of Krispy Kreme donuts, and a son with Down syndrome, before I would really fall in love with that little girl.

> *"The great thing about getting older is that you don't have to
> lose all the other ages you've been."*
> ~ Madeleine L'Engle ~

3.

BIRTHDAYS

We celebrated James' first birthday with friends and family.
I wanted just one photo of him diving into his birthday cupcake,
devouring the frosting, like in photos I'd seen of other one-year-
olds. But he wouldn't touch it. I wanted him to get buried in the

paper of his gifts. But he wouldn't go near them. I wanted him to do *anything* that might resemble knowing it was his birthday. But he was happiest when we left him alone in his room. And so was I.

After James was born there was always someone staying in our guest room, dubbed The Marshmallow Room because of its comfy king-size bed and all-white down cover. They said they were coming to see James, but in hindsight I know they were coming to check up on me. Depression had moved in, like a thief, sneaky and robbing. And I was not in good shape. If I didn't have to be in the studio or if I wasn't out on the road performing, I usually didn't get out of bed. Suicidal thoughts circled inside my head like hawks on roadkill.

I reluctantly started a friendship with a few other families who had children with Down syndrome. Terri and Steve Argo invited us over for dinner one night, to meet their daughter Olivia, who was about four years old at the time. I didn't want to go.

Terri greeted us at the door. My first thought was, "Well, she doesn't look depressed or overwhelmed. She's actually very attractive and dresses cute." And then Olivia came running into the foyer and I felt like I had been slapped in the face. She was wearing the most adorable red and white outfit covered in ladybugs. Her hair was neatly pulled back into a ponytail. And her spirit and smile could hardly be contained. But it took every inch of strength I had to hold back the tears. All I could see and feel was my own fear.

It was hard to keep the calendar straight as to which therapist — speech, occupational or physical — was coming on which day for a session with James. It started to feel like it had in my house growing up, except now people weren't coming to drink, but to work. Although most days I would have gladly poured a few mojitos if they were interested. The therapists were all very nice, but occasionally one of them would try to teach me. They would say something like, "You know, Lynn, the red ball would really be better at motivating him than the blue ball."

I would stare at them and smile. What I wanted to say was, "I don't care which ball is better. That is your job, not mine. I've barely signed on for motherhood; being a therapist as well is not on my list."

One day, Kelly, his occupational therapist at the time, showed up a bit early for her scheduled appointment. She caught me off guard, still in my pink robe, just finishing up my morning crying session.

She made her way to James' room and I ran around the house picking up dirty clothes and Fido's toys. A bit later I heard James screaming at the top of his lungs. I went to check in on them, and when I opened the door she was swinging him around the room in a sling contraption over-the-shoulder thingy. She assured me it was safe and she was trying to tame his sensitivity issues. Although I couldn't help but wonder if it was why he *had* sensitivity issues.

She asked if I was okay. I was going to lie but then I caught a glimpse of myself in the mirror and realized my morning tears had caused yesterday's mascara to leave the dreaded black tracks on my face. Clearly I was not okay. There are those moments in life when if you're not in a good place emotionally and someone just looks at you with the wee bit of concern, you will turn into a pile of mush. And that's what I did. She listened and swung James, and over his cries and mine, she told me she had a great therapist named Diane and would gladly give me her number.

It had been a few years since I was in therapy. Part of me was sure I had worked through all my issues years ago with Bob, and next with a lady named Beth and then with another woman named Betty. I learned so much about the disease of alcoholism and its effects on me. I learned to set up emotional boundaries with my father and I would no longer let him cross those lines. I screamed and yelled at my dead mother for months until I was hoarse. I understood what it meant to be a codependent, and I thought I was done being one.

But understanding your hurts and actually healing them are two completely different things.

I had plenty of head knowledge, but my heart was still protected by a thick layer of shame. I knew I wasn't happy, maybe even knew I was depressed, but I had good reason to be. I had a son with Down syndrome. What could a therapist do about that?

I picked up the phone and made an appointment for the next week.

Diane was an attractive woman in her fifties, with shoulder-length brunette hair and a great smile. She seemed extremely comfortable in her own skin. I complimented her on the strapless dress she was wearing. She said, "You know, I didn't wear strapless dresses until I was in my forties because as a young girl my mother told me they didn't look good on me. Then one day I tried one on and I realized she was wrong."

Her office was in an old house outside of Nashville. It was small and cozy, with a brown leather sofa, ivory throw blanket, a wall full of books and a box of Kleenex. I fiddled with the fringe on the blanket as I talked, trying to untangle each tassel. I told her everything I believed was my problem. "I was raised with an alcoholic father and I still struggle with those issues sometimes. I'm not sure what I even believe about God and feel guilty for even thinking that. I'm totally pissed at anyone resembling a Pentecostal/Charismatic Christian. My husband and I are on two different pages about almost everything. I have a six-month-old son who was born with Down syndrome. Oh, and most days I don't want to be alive anymore, and the only relief I feel is when I think about being dead."

"That's a lot," she said. "I think we're gonna have to prioritize." Not necessarily what you want to hear from your therapist. But then she said, "First things first, let's get you on an antidepressant."

I laughed in her face. "No way!" I said. I told her I came from a family of drug addicts and we frowned on any type of drug use. I told her I was always the person trying to convince other people not to go on an antidepressant because it would just cover up the problem. That they needed to suck it up and get to therapy and understand whatever was wrong. And mostly I assured her that I knew deep down I could fix everything. I just needed her to tell me how to keep hiding and arranging and running. She looked at me a bit funny.

She said she believed my brain was no longer producing enough serotonin and the antidepressant would give it a little boost. She also told me I wouldn't have to be on it for life, just long enough to help myself dig through the muddy parts. And she told me she didn't much care for the Pentecostals either. And then she said, "Lynn, if you were to be diagnosed with diabetes, would you take insulin to stay alive?

I thought of my friend Jillian.

Jillian and I work together in television. I love the industry, and I've had a dual love affair between television production and music my whole life. I started working in TV in college and went on to become a freelance assistant director and producer. I feel at home in the madness. Every production office may as well be my kitchen growing up, with people running around playing their parts, doing their jobs, trying to control chaos.

Jillian is a line producer, so she handles any and all of the logistics that go into a production. She is an adorable petite blonde, with a ton of energy and an infectious spirit. Most days she wears jeans and great cowboy boots. And every day she wears a diabetic pump. It's keeping her alive.

One time we were working together on a comedy show at The Mirage Hotel and Casino in Vegas. When I arrived at the makeshift production office in the theater, I immediately felt the energy swirling about. A storm was brewing and Jillian was in the midst of trying to control the chaos. She's great at it, but she's had practice. In her first career she was a schoolteacher. She also had to grow up quick. She lost her mom to suicide when she was only two. Actually, she lost her mom to depression first. Suicide was just the visible result. When we met, we bonded over the fact that we both lost our moms and neither of us were sure we wanted kids. Plus, she's from Michigan, which means she gets how it feels to be a northerner stuck in the middle of the Bible Belt.

As the crisis in the production office escalated—and I use the word "crisis" with liberty here, because it was about finding a stunt bunny or the fact the costumes for the dogs weren't quite right or we were out of Twizzlers on the craft service table or maybe it was about a real security issue. I can't remember—Jillian had it all under control.

In the height of the madness, she discretely reached down to her side, took out the small device, pushed a button and put it away, all the while continuing to talk on the phone and send an email. This didn't surprise me because I've known for years she is a diabetic. And what she did in those few seconds kept her alive. But what I understood that day was Jillian's ability to accept what she had been given. She embraced what she has and in return she gets to live.

I took Diane's advice, and started taking Lexapro. It turned out to be one of the best reluctant choices I made on my journey to getting well.

Sometimes it's the things we try to run the furthest away from that can start to bring us home.

My weekly visits with Diane also taught me that when you are not in a good place, when all you can do is cry, you need to find someone you trust. A friend or a therapist who is not acting crazy like you are at the moment. And you need to listen to whatever they say, even if it goes against what you believe. The odds are good that they are making better decisions than you are at the moment.

It took a while for the Lexapro to kick in, but I did feel slightly better. At least I wasn't crying every day. And I committed to meeting with Diane every week. I was shocked to realize how many wounds were still buried inside. How many issues I thought I had worked through that still needed attention. Not to mention, being a mom brought up a ton of issues in regards to my mother. I was realizing how much I was like her, how much I still didn't understand her, and how much I still needed her. Diane said,

"We remember stories from our past when we are ready. When our hearts are able to handle the truth and accept them for what they truly were."

~

I lay on our plaid couch with my feet resting in my mom's lap. I pulled the brown and orange striped afghan closer to my nose, smelling the yarn as the smoke lingered above my head. *General Hospital* played on the television. She took her right hand and gently rubbed my feet, up and down and up and down. Her one hand large enough to cover both feet, leaving her left hand free to smoke. I was three years old; this is my first real memory of mom.

She spent her days doing. In the summertime you would find her in the backyard, tending to the pool filter, cussing under her breath as water sprayed her floral smock. Or standing in the driveway with the hose, watering the flowers she planted and loved. In the winter, she would put on her green coat with the fur hood and work gloves and spend hours in the cold changing the bulbs of our elaborate display of Christmas lights. And when she was done, she would sit at the barstool at the kitchen counter and stare out the window. With a cup of coffee that had been reheated on stove and a cigarette, she would click her strong unkempt fingernails on the kitchen counter to a melody that played only in her head. I always wondered what she was waiting for.

My mom took care of everybody. My dad, extended family members, neighbors and strangers. The year our neighbor Mr. Bergman lost his job, my mom bought the Christmas presents for all five of his kids. And whenever anyone asked to borrow money, she gave more than they needed and never kept a record. But I know it was harder for her to be as loving to her own children. Her words were short and to the point and often cold. She rarely called me Lynn, but preferred Kid instead. She chose her battles, lost many, but won a few too. She was a survivor, and that was the first thing she taught me to be.

It was March 1965 and my mom's due date was still two months away. She started hemorrhaging at home and they rushed her to the hospital. My sister Kathy, just fourteen at the time, said she had never seen so much blood.

The doctor told my father that my mom was close to death and she might not make it. "I don't think I can save them both. I'm assuming you want the priority to be your wife?" My dad said yes. My life at the moment lay in the hands of a young Asian doctor. They did an emergency C-section and immediately called for the priest. I was given my last rites, the Catholic sacrament that you receive on your deathbed. This is a comforting thought for me, because if it ends up that the Catholics were the ones who had it right, then I will have already partaken in the most important sacrament of them all. I'm covered. A day later, to everyone's surprise, I was still breathing when the hospital administrator brought in the birth papers to sign.

My father said, "We decided on Kimberly Marie, correct?"

My mom said, "No. I've changed my mind. I want to name her LynnMarie, in honor of the doctor that saved her."

Thank you, Dr. Linn, for working so hard to keep me alive that March morning.

Thirty years later, when the Internet was just making its way into daily life, I received a letter in the mail. It was from a man in France who wrote; *"Dear LynnMarie, Enclosed please find a photo of our first born daughter – LynnMarie. We found your music on line and it has brought us so much joy. Can you please tell us how you got your name so we can tell our daughter how she got hers?"* I wrote him back and told him the story. I told him how much I loved my name and the name carried an innate desire for survival.

I used to love hearing my dad tell the story about my arrival. His animated tones and tossing between anger and joy reminded me that I caused a big commotion, which I of course, secretly loved. My dad says that when he held me for the first time, at two pounds, eight ounces, I was so small I fit in the palm of his hand.

I think this is why out of all the Bible verses my favorite is Isaiah 49:15 -16, "…but even if that were possible, I would not forget you! See, I have written your name on the palms of my hands" (New Living Translation). Both my earthly father and God, holding me in the palm of their hands. This is a comforting mental picture when I feel that God has taken a break from me. That all my rants and raves and complaints got to be too much for Him and He has His iPod on high and is ignoring my requests.

My dad did not sugarcoat his words. He always told it like it was. He said I was ugly. That my skin was paper thin, so thin you could see through it. And that I was born without fingernails and eyebrows or eyelashes. My siblings said I looked like a rat and no one wanted to hold me. This is why the first photo of me wasn't taken until I was six months old. It's odd to have no documentation of the first six months of your life.

I was strong enough to be removed from the incubator eight weeks later. But if it wasn't for a friend of my father, I may have become a resident of Cleveland General Hospital. My father was handed a bill for over $300,000, which would be about one million dollars today. My dad said, "Look, I don't have it. So I guess you can keep her," and left the hospital without me.

What?! You're leaving? Are you serious? I just fought like hell to be here and you're walking out on me? He didn't have the money. He sunk every dime he had into buying his bar, so this—meaning a sick child—was not part of his plan.

In the end, my father's friend who owned his own construction business finagled a way to put my dad on the payroll so he could qualify for insurance. They also fudged the dates of the fake employment so it looked like my dad was covered when I was born. I hate that all these shenanigans went on around my birth, and I'm hoping the statute of limitations on insurance fraud is shorter than forty-five years.

My older cousins tell me my mom hid her pregnancy from everyone except my father. I wish I knew why this was. So both my arrival and survival were a shock to the family as well as a reason to celebrate, which they did. They had a welcome home party, first for my mom, then for me. Then a baptismal party. They bought me doll clothes from Kresge's Department Store because they didn't make baby clothes small enough to fit me. And they diapered me with a hanky. This all seems so wrong in some ways. So fragile. So breakable. Back then they didn't save babies like me. I shouldn't be here. But somehow, and for some reason, my mom and I both survived.

Years later I asked my sister Kathy's best friend, Brenda, who spent most of her high school years in our house, (and who would have been sixteen when I was born), "What do you think my mom was feeling when I came home from the hospital?" She took a long time to answer. "Perplexed and distressed."

4.

KARIE

In the very popular 1982 book *The Birth Order*, Kevin Leman writes, *"Middle children often have the feeling that they are ignored in*

favor of their older and younger siblings," which pretty much sums it up. I believe my sister Karie loved and loathed me growing up, and probably still does at times.

Karie is five years older than me. Her real name was Karen Rose. But Grandma JoHana didn't like it and nicknamed her Karica, which became Karie. She's tall and slender, way too thin, and has a great smile, although she doesn't think so. As kids she was always the one ordered to watch out for me, drive me to and from my cheerleading practices, and clean up after me. She was my guide through the awkward years of puberty. She taught me how to shave my legs and pluck my eyebrows. We lost contact for a few years while I was away at Oral Roberts University and newly married, because I was told I needed to distance myself from a family that would not understand my love for Jesus. But once I started playing my accordion again, she came to every gig, stood in the front row and cheered louder than anyone.

She came to Nashville a lot when I was pregnant and for the first few years of James' life. Actually my father would send her. "Go fix your sister," he'd say. And, like the good codependent she was, she would put her own life and needs on hold to come care for me. She'd come and clean my house and wash my clothes and take care of James. My house would be so clean when she left you could eat off the kitchen floor. But when something gets that clean it just shows you how dirty everything else is.

Having her around was also a reminder to me how I was failing at motherhood. I was such as mess and so covered up in depression that there were times she thought she'd have to adopt my son. And I couldn't help but wonder if he would have done better living with her. She had two kids by the time she was twenty-one. She knew how to get on the floor with them and make a whole production out of a shoebox, some string and a sock. I can barely figure out how to open the stroller.

But Karie's strengths were birthed out of her struggles and her secrets. She too spent her whole life running and hiding. Leman also says, *"Middle children lean towards having personalities that are secretive."*

~

It was the winter of 1977 and Cleveland was in the middle of one of the worst ice storms in its history. Six-foot-long icicles hung from the awnings, covering our windows like bars on a jail cell. The city was paralyzed and stayed frozen for over two weeks. Schools were cancelled and stores were closed. Karie was only seventeen that January, a junior in high school, when one night at midnight, she woke up my mom.

"Mom, I'm having a baby. Right now."

Karie and her boyfriend had sex for the first time on prom night the previous spring. And she spent the following nine months hiding her pregnancy. No one knew. I know, it's one of those things that from the outside looking in you say, "Come on, how could no one have seen it?" I don't know. But we didn't. Or maybe we chose not to see it. With enough dysfunction in a house, things don't appear as they are. Karie was a cheerleader while she was pregnant. She did a thousand sit-ups a night. It was the late seventies and baby doll tops were in style. So she lived in denial. Maybe we all lived in denial. Until we couldn't anymore.

My mom said, "You call your father at the bar and you tell him; you tell him I hurt my back and I can't get up and he needs to come home now."

Karie shook as she dialed the number. We never called my father at the bar.

"God dammit, I can't come home now!" he screamed and hung up on her.

She lay on the floor, in the midst of a contraction, with the dial tone blaring in her ear. Her next call was to her boyfriend. He and his parents drove through the ice. It took them forty-five minutes to travel three miles. They put Karie in the car and another hour and a half later finally made it to the nearby hospital. She delivered a baby boy within minutes of arriving.

My dad showed up in her hospital room the next day at noon, on a break from the bar, and the only thing he said to her was, "You will put this baby up for adoption and we will never speak of it again."

And we didn't.

There was no way my father was going to let this baby ruin his reputation. He was Lud Hrovat. Lud Hrovat who owned Lud's

Tavern on Libby Road. His family was perfect. These things didn't happen to us. If people knew about this, how would that make him look? And so the problem went away.

I was eleven at the time, and all I remember is waking up in the middle of the night and hearing commotion downstairs in the kitchen. But this was normal. Often times I'd be awakened to hear people drunk downstairs, stopping by to borrow money or a case of beer out of our garage. So, I fell back to sleep and was told in the morning that Karie was in the hospital with stomach problems. I didn't ask any questions. We never asked questions. And when she came home a few days later, I was told to stay away from her, as if she was infectious and being near her would make me a sinner too. And then, a few weeks after that, without even saying goodbye, she was gone. Sent eight hundred miles away to spend some time with my brother Larry.

I was never told she had a baby.

While Karie was visiting Larry, my father had his first heart attack. He was fifty years old and fell into an alcohol withdrawal-induced coma. The doctors said that the chances of his survival were slim and if he did survive, he would be a vegetable. At least that's what I overheard my mom say to Larry over the phone. Karie and Larry flew home the next day to be a part of the new crisis.

Seven years later, as I packed up my room to leave for college, Karie came in and sat on the end of my bed. For some reason, she thought this was the right time to tell me that I had another nephew. I couldn't even grasp what she was saying. "How could you or they or anyone not tell me? How could you lie to me all these years?"

I remember feeling so cheated, so left out. Like I wasn't invited to the party. I was shocked that I didn't know. Shocked that everyone could keep such a secret. And if they could lie about that, what else was not true? All of a sudden nothing was real. And then so many things made sense. Like why my parents freaked out when I got asked to prom my sophomore year. I was a good kid; the boy was a good boy. Why were they questioning whether or not I should be allowed to go? Now I understood their fear. And then my anger got focused on my dad. How could he give his grandchild away? This was one more reason why I couldn't wait to leave for college and get away from my father.

~

My new smoking habit covered my dorm room at Bowling Green State University with a thin grayish sheen, making everything around me look like it was old and dying. To say I was lost and confused would be an understatement. BGSU was known as a party school and I dove in headfirst. Within the  first two weeks I was a mess. I started drinking almost daily at noon. I rarely went to class. I did a 180-degree turn from the girl I was in high school. At Lake Catholic High School, I was motivated and focused and involved. I was on every committee possible and had the lead in every high school play. I couldn't believe how quickly that girl was gone.

Months went by and things got progressively worse. Dirty clothes piled up on my floor until there was no more room to walk. My girlfriend Chris, who lived next door, came in one day and found me in the fetal position in my bed, listening to the Bread song "Everything I Own" on repeat. I missed my mom so much.

She abruptly lifted the needle off the record player, which I was sure was going to leave a scratch. She opened the curtains, letting in a stream of light. Then, what happened next was one of the most tangible examples of the life of Jesus I had ever personally experienced. She carried seven loads of laundry down two flights of stairs and paid over ten bucks (a lot of money in college) to wash my clothes. That day, it wasn't about why I was flunking Theater 101, it wasn't about figuring out if I had a drinking problem and it wasn't about dealing with the pain I was feeling over my mother's death just eight months prior. That day, it was about dirty underwear. And by washing my clothes she gave me more hope than anything else could have.

I was feeling slightly better, and somehow found the strength to go to an audition. I got the lead in one of the small fall drama productions. But a few weeks into rehearsals, when I found out I would have to kiss a black man, I withdrew. I told the director that I no longer wanted to be on stage. I knew he would never understand that my father would kill me if I kissed a black man. And truthfully, I had been raised in such a racist home, I didn't know if I could kiss a black man. In hindsight, this lost opportunity reveals what narrow-mindedness and shame can make you believe.

It's difficult to prosper when you are at a place you know you're not supposed to be. Nothing will work. No matter how hard you try, doors will close and windows will not open. Everything will be difficult. Besides the fact I was walking around carrying so much grief and confusion over Karie's baby and my mother's death, I was not succeeding because I didn't really want to be there. Bowling Green was the easy choice, my dad's choice, but not where my heart wanted to be. Where I wanted to go, where I believed I would have thrived, I couldn't get to. There was too much fear, dysfunction and grief standing in the way.

It was about a month after my mom had died that my dad came home and saw my acceptance letter on the kitchen table, mixed in with all the sympathy cards. It was an invitation to audition at the American Academy of Dramatic Arts in New York City. My drama coach at the time, Mrs. Paulett, had sent in the paperwork without me knowing. My dad looked at me and in a very disgusted voice said, "Eh, LynnMarie, there's one of you, from every high school and every city and every state. What makes you think you can do this acting thing?"

What I wanted to say was, "Because I know I can." Or at least Mrs. Paulett thinks I can. What I wanted to say was, "I want to be an entertainer, just like you. I knew at seven years old from watching you that I belonged on stage." But nothing came out. I had no words. And the mean voices arrived in my head. "Obviously you are not good enough to do this. Maybe you are not talented at all. You think you can, but maybe you're wrong. You are wrong!"

What I know now, after a lifetime of therapy and chocolate, is that the external me, the one who won acting and music awards, she wanted to succeed. From the outside it looked as if she could do anything she wanted to. But the internal me was so messed up from not having a sense of self that I didn't even know where to begin. When your opportunity to make decisions for yourself is stripped away, the ability to learn your inner voice and know your own desires also goes away. My mother would say to me, "Kid, I entered you in a button accordion contest this weekend and I bought you a new outfit to wear and you should play "Visoko Nad Oblaki"." And I would. And I would win.

I spent my entire life not having to make any decisions. My mom did it for me.

She didn't do this to be mean; she did it so she had control so nothing could go wrong, as to not upset my father. So how could I possibly make such a big decision as college when I didn't even pick out my own clothes?

But my dad wasn't any better off in knowing who he was than I was. It was like the blind leading the blind. In therapy with Bob, I went back and sat next to the teenage girl at that kitchen table. And I told her, "Here's the deal. You are not wrong. You really should be going to New York. But what your father doesn't know how to say is that he's scared and lonely. His wife just died and you're all he's got left, and if he loses you he doesn't know what he will do. So it's easier for him to convince you to go to Bowling Green than it is to support your dream and have you leave town."

We don't realize as kids that, while we are growing up, our parents are trying to figure out their own stuff at the same time. They are dealing with mid-life crises and financial woes and relationship problems, all the while they are trying to parent. And in my dad's case, he was dealing with insurmountable loss. He could never have had my best interests at heart at the time.

As my first year of college went on, I drank as much as I could. Drinking allowed me to not feel. But by spring just drinking wasn't enough. Clothes get dirty again.

Once the drug you're using to cover your pain no longer works, you will find something else and up the ante, because feeling is not an option just yet.

~

The weather warmed up and there were news reports that there was a rapist on campus. Several girls had been attacked. The University set up a "Buddy Walk" program so no girl would be walking across campus alone at night. But I never called the hotline.
Instead, I would set my alarm for 1 a.m. and I would walk the campus aimlessly for hours. In my crazy mind, being raped would have been easier to deal with. It would have been a tangible reason to be depressed and sad and get me the attention I so desperately needed.

I lived for the weekends when friends would come to visit. Karen came to celebrate my nineteenth birthday. Karen Aveni and I have been friends since freshman year at Lake Catholic High School. She is small and Italian, and has beautiful thick dark hair and dark eyes. We met within the first week of school, and she stayed my friend even though I called her Mary for almost a month. That describes Karen perfectly. Easygoing. Non-confrontational. And lets her loud bossy friend be loud and bossy.

After doing way too many shots at Dino's, we walked out the front door of the bar to head back to my dorm room. We had barely stepped off the curb and into the crosswalk when it happened. In the rain and darkness we never even saw the white Volkswagen Rabbit. The seconds that followed the impact happened in slow motion. I heard each one of my limbs hit and then bounce off the car. I tumbled over the roof and landed in the middle of the intersection. When I hit the pavement time returned to normal speed. I felt the hard cement. I tasted the rain. My first thought was sadness that I was still alive. A crowd of kids gathered around us. I searched for my shoes in the street.

"Karen! Karen?!" I yelled.

Karen was thrown about twenty feet and landed on the other side of the intersection. But she was alright too. We hugged and, because we were drunk, we started laughing. The driver of the car begged us to let him take us to the hospital. There was no way in hell we could go to the hospital, even though I did have on clean underwear. First of all, we were drunk, and second of all, Karen's mom would never survive such a phone call. You see, Karen had to beg Mrs. Aveni to even let her come to visit me. Because twenty years earlier Mrs. Aveni's sister-in-law was killed in a car crash in Bowling Green.

There are people who know things. Karen's mom is one of them. The only time I ever got in real trouble in high school was when Mrs. Aveni *knew* we weren't where we said we'd be and busted us for having a hotel room party all night. Mrs. Aveni knows how to listen to her inner voice.

Miraculously, Karen and I walked away from that accident with only external bruises. This was one time that alcohol saved my life. We were so relaxed our bodies tumbled like gymnasts.

The semester ended, I was still alive, and I packed up my dorm room and planned on spending the summer in Cleveland before returning to BGSU in the fall. My dad and I weren't on good terms at this point; maybe it had something to do with my 1.4 GPA. I don't know. Maybe he was drinking as much as I was. But I knew I was in bad shape and gravely disappointing him when he said, "I'm thinking that instead of coming home, maybe you should go spend some time with your brother Larry."

My friends, having heard stories all year about my brother in Tulsa said, "You're gonna go visit and come back one of those crazy, bible-thumping, hell-is-real born again Christians."

"No way," I said. "Never."

5.

ROOTS

Michael Hrovat and JoHana Vidic, my grandparents, came
to the USA in 1908. They came separately, and both settled in the
Newburgh area of Cleveland, just a few blocks from one another.
On one of my visits to Slovenia I discovered that they lived close to

each other there too. Michael grew up on one side of the Krka River in the village of Zagradec, and JoHana on the other in Drašča Vas. My relatives also told me that Michael was a shoemaker in Slovenia before he came to America. And that when he made a pair of shoes for himself, he would carve an M on his left sole and an H on his right. He wanted people to know where he had walked and that "Michael Hrovat had been there." I love this story and it reminds me how important it is to try to leave our mark on this world.

Michael and JoHana met just weeks after their arrival in Cleveland. Michael told his brother Frank, "Give me six weeks and I will marry that beautiful girl, and if I don't, you can have my watch." This was a bold statement on his part because his watch was

his only possession worth anything. He got the girl, kept the watch and they had eleven children. Those eleven children had twenty-three children and those children had too many children to count.

The Hrovats, circa 1947

After they were married, they built the little white house on Stanley Avenue. You couldn't throw a rock without hitting a Hrovat. Auntie Jennie and her kids lived on one side of us, my grandparents on the other. (We lived in the house my grandfather built and lived in, until he built a new house right next door.) And just a few streets away were Auntie Olga and Auntie Rosie and Uncle Joe.

Hrovat is a very common name in Slovenia and not so uncommon in Cleveland. If you say it correctly, it should sound like you are about to hurl as the word gathers in the back of your throat and moves over your tongue and through your lips. Hhhhhrovat. But with each generation the pronunciation became more American. "It's Hrovat, with a silent H," I would say.

My grandparents spoke Slovenian and very little English. Their children spoke some Slovenian, but they wanted them to be as American as possible. By the time my generation came around I only learned the important Slovenian phrases, like how to tell someone to go to hell or that they were full of shit. But I started singing in Slovenian as soon as I could talk. On Saturday mornings I would sit in the front row at The Nash with other neighbor kids and Auntie Olga would teach us Slovenian folk songs. She would go through every word of each song, explaining the meaning, and making sure we pronounced it just right. "Rože" for flowers, with a rolled R. This care and cultivation, carved out a place in my heart for all things Slovenian—the food, the culture, the music.

In America, my grandfather was a brick maker by day and a bootlegger all the time. During prohibition he distilled and sold 100-proof, plum-flavored grain alcohol— Slivovica —out of the basement of his house. One day three men from the FBI came by and forced their way in, in a scene I imagined to have gone down like something resembling Sean Connery in *The Untouchables*. With their rifles waving, they pushed my grandmother aside as they entered the house and headed to the basement.

She stood by helpless, watching them pour lye into the huge wooden vats, ruining the process, and leaving an obvious calling card that said, "This production is officially shut down. You will no longer make whiskey in this house."

When my grandfather got home from work that night, he started skimming the tops of the big, round barrels. JoHana said, "Michael, what are you doing? They have shut us down!"

He said, "Yes, but they're not coming back today. So today, I'm making whiskey." He was resilient.

My grandmother was resilient too. "Strong like bull," was her favorite saying, and she was. She birthed eleven kids on a kitchen table. A kitchen table! I had one kid, drugged up, in a hospital bed, and by Cesarean section and I couldn't get out of my robe.

If you take away the alcoholism and the codependency and the fear, we had an idyllic childhood. We had games of hide-n-seek that spanned the length of four yards. We played moon dog in the street and running bases on the sidewalk. On hot summer days we swam in our backyard pool or in the stream of water when they flushed the fire hydrants. And we got Screwballs and Bomb Pops from Uncle Marty's Ice Cream Truck every afternoon.

We continued the traditions that the immigrants brought over. Especially around the holidays. I think I was in my early teens before I realized that not everyone circled their house on Holy Saturday morning carrying a basket of blessed horseradish.

My mom would fill our best Easter basket with a tiny bit of everything we were going to eat at Sunday's Easter meal. Ham, klobasi, eggs, homemade bread, salt and horseradish. She would cover it with the prettiest doily, one handmade by Grandma JoHana. Then I would walk up to The Nash, where a priest would bless our food. The tradition dates back to the 15th century when Slavic people abstained from eating meat and eggs during Lent, and now it was time to indulge again. And they hoped the church's blessing on the food would prove a remedy for whatever harmful effects the body might have suffered from the long period of self-denial.

Somewhere in the handing down of traditions, it was added that a stroll around your house would help reinforce the blessing. I carried that basket and that blessed horseradish around and around the house, hoping that somehow it would make me feel less afraid and more loved.

As we got older, each of us six siblings settled into our roles. We had them all. The addict, the hero, the scapegoat, the mascot, the lost child and the caretaker.

Larry was without a doubt the family hero. An extremely good-looking kid with dark inset eyes and broad shoulders. Whenever he walked in the house the party began. He was a high school football star and probably on the verge of becoming an alcoholic. I remember the way it felt when he would pick me up with one hand and hold me over his head. Occasionally he and Lenny would let me play in the pool with them and they would throw me so high in the air it seemed as if it took minutes to fall back into the water. He was strong, and extremely charismatic. He almost got expelled three days before graduation from Chanel High School because he threatened to hurt the Mechanical Drawing teacher. Instead, he threw desks and drawing boards out the third story window. When my dad went to the principal and begged him to let Larry graduate the principal said, "Mr. Hrovat, I don't think you know how much power your son has. If Larry Hrovat stood outside those doors at 3 p.m. and told everyone to stay home tomorrow, no one would show up for school." I'm guessing my dad paid him off, because Larry did end up graduating.

He was recruited to play for football for legendary coach Bear Bryant at the University of Alabama in 1970, until he got caught cheating on his SATs. He obviously didn't make the wisest choice when he paid the smartest kid in the class to take the test for him. He ended up playing football for a junior college in Kansas instead. But in his sophomore year, he says he met Jesus in a country church. He quit drinking and eventually entered the seminary at Oral Roberts University.

It was the seventies and the height of the charismatic Jesus movement. Larry dove in head first. From the outside looking in it seemed he just switched drugs. Alcohol was out – Jesus was in. He was the first person in hundreds of years of Catholicism in our family to believe something different. And that was a hard pill to swallow.

He and his wife Debbie would come back to Cleveland to visit, and it was always bittersweet. We were so happy to see them, and usually another new baby or two. But the visits always got rocky. Combining the differences in spiritual beliefs was like trying to mix oil and water.

Larry would walk outside to the apple trees that lined my grandfather's backyard. He would pick a branch, not too thick and not too long, and strip it clean of leaves. And then, behind closed doors, we'd hear the beatings. "Spare the rod, spoil the child" was the bible verse they quoted. My mom and dad would pace in the kitchen, knowing it wasn't their place to step in. I couldn't figure out which God was worse—the Catholic God who, if I had sex or lied, was going to send me to hell, or the Born Again God who, if I didn't accept Jesus with my whole heart (and apparently discipline my children with a switch), was going to send me to hell.

It was obvious to me that my parents didn't agree with Larry's actions, but they must have thought something about his newfound faith was good. Because if anyone was ever in trouble, they got sent to Larry.

~

It was May and already hot in Tulsa. I spent my days lying in the sun on the basketball courts outside graduate housing where Larry, Debbie and their five children were living. (I had to lie out in shorts and a T-shirt because a bathing suit would be too promiscuous.) I was good at lying in the sun. At the end of the year at Bowling Green, our floor gave out awards and I got "Lies in the Sun the Most." I'm pretty sure they didn't know what else to give me. Cries the most? Sleeps until noon the most? Most likely to get raped?

I managed to make it through the whole visit without anything voodoo-ish happening to me. But then, on the eve of my departure, Larry asked me if I'd like to go to a healing service they were holding on the campus of Oral Roberts University. I had no idea what a healing service was, but I said yes. And I don't know why. Maybe I was so desperate to stop hurting that I thought being around *those people* would at least make me feel better.

But, one foot into the service and I agreed with my friends — these were crazy people! They were jumping up and down and speaking in what I would learn was "tongues", weeping and carrying on, sprawled out all over the floor. I was scared. I was freaked out. So I left. I went out the side door and then through another door and stumbled into the ORU Chapel.

It was completely dark inside, except for one stage light. I walked to the middle of that room and I sat in a pew and I stared up at the cross. I quietly said, "Look, I don't even know if you're real. I don't know if I even believe in you. But I do know that I am a mess and I need help. So, if you are listening, and if you care, can you help me?"

There were no bells and whistles. There were no fireworks and no angels singing. There was only silence. And then a knowing. A deep, deep knowing that yes, there was something more than just what I could see or touch. Something bigger than myself.

I walked out of the chapel and a back into the crazy room. I stepped over a woman lying on the floor. I sat in the first empty seat I could find. I was crying. An elderly woman sitting next to me handed me her white hanky, embroidered with lilac and yellow flowers, and asked me what was wrong.

I told her, "I'm not sure, but I think I may have just found God."

What I didn't realize at the time was everyone in that room was on a mission. They all knew I was Larry's "unsaved" little sister from Ohio. And as it would turn out, the woman I sat next to was married to the man on stage and they must have had some secret mode of communication because suddenly the preacher said in his low-toned dramatic voice, "You know, an amazing thing happened here tonight—a young lady got saved. I wish she would come up here."

I started looking around the room, thinking "Oh my gosh! Where is the sucker? Someone actually fell for this shit?"

But nobody stood up.

Then he turned and pointed directly at me, and said, "If she won't come up here, I wish she would just raise her hand." The room stood still. The pressure mounted. Everyone was staring at me. It was the most uncomfortable moment I'd ever felt. And then, as if it wasn't connected to my own body, I watched my left hand lift from my thigh.

The next thing I knew I was on stage; my brother came up crying, everyone was cheering and waving their hands in the air, and I just wanted to scream out, "But wait, nothing happened to me!" But it was too late. The train had already left the station. According to everyone in that room, I was now a full-fledged, card-carrying member of the "Born Again Christian Club". I hate clubs. In an instant, they took the precious personal moment I had in that chapel and categorized it. They turned it into what they needed it to be. A few minutes earlier, I had felt peace and love, and now I felt confusion and pressure. At the same time, I have to be honest that a small part of me loved being up on that stage and getting the attention. I was being hugged and cared for and welcomed. And that felt good. It was the first time I had felt anything good in years. So I held on tight.

I was scheduled to fly back to the Cleveland the next morning. Larry suggested that I delay my flight and give myself some time to get "strong in my faith" before I headed back to a family of non-believers. And I also needed to be "filled with the Holy Spirit".

The Pentecostal/Charismatics, of which my brother was one, believe that a "second experience" after conversion is available to Christians. Not every Christian does it, but every Christian should; and until he or she does, no Christian can walk in "the power" of the Spirit. The evidence of this second experience is speaking with other tongues (although not all Charismatics are agreed on this point).

Of course I didn't know any of this and even if I did, I wouldn't have been able to understand it—hell, I don't even understand it now, but Larry did and I trusted him. If I stayed, and got "filled with the Holy Spirit" I would be strong enough to stay a Christian and not be wooed by the evil ways of my family, and thus never get to heaven. It turns out that you can't get to heaven by way of Cleveland.

So I stayed in Tulsa. And a few days later I attended what they called a Camp Meeting. I sat in the second row of the auditorium feeling like a stranger in a strange land. I was surrounded by people in wheelchairs and on crutches. A very popular preacher was speaking that night on the power of faith. I didn't understand a lot of what he said, but then he said something that I did understand. He pointed directly at a little girl who was lying on a gurney in the front row—her head two sizes too big—and said, "If you are not healed tonight it is because of *your* lack of faith."

I was so angry. How could he say that to that little girl?

Out in the lobby after the service I was full of questions. None of what I just saw and experienced seemed to make sense to me. I begged the new friends I was with for answers about the little girl. They gathered around me and said, "Lynn, there are things in life that only the spirit can understand. Until you are filled with the Holy Spirit, none of this will make sense." They formed a circle around me, laid their hands on me, and started to pray. And they were not going to stop until I would speak in tongues. We stood for well over forty-five minutes. My left leg was falling asleep. My stomach was growling. I thought I might pass out. And it wasn't working.

"Just stop!" I wanted to yell, "Just stop!" But I said nothing. Desperate to have it end, I mumbled a few words in Slovenian. They erupted in cheers. The Holy Spirit had arrived.

Larry drove me to the airport the next day. He gave me all kinds of advice, based on his experience, on how to explain my salvation and how the family was not going to understand my newfound love for Jesus. And then he said, "You know, Lynn, you might want to re-evaluate your desire to be on stage or play the accordion. The accordion promotes dancing and drinking and it could really mess with your eternal life."

When I got home my dad and I were hardly speaking. And with my mom gone, I needed someone to be my caretaker. I needed someone to tell me what to do and where to go and how to dress. I needed to be codependent. Larry didn't ask for the job, maybe didn't even know he was doing it, but I clung to his words and did everything he suggested.

I put the accordion in the closet. I started trying to be a good Christian. I started reading the Bible. I broke up with my high school boyfriend because I was told we were now "unequally yoked". I quit smoking and drinking. And I didn't dare tell anyone that I still felt empty. I wanted so badly for it all to be real.

Then, I did the only thing I could do. I transferred to Oral Roberts University.

> *"Every happening, great and small, is a parable whereby God*
> *speaks to us, and the art of life is to get the message."*
> ~ Malcolm Muggeridge ~

6.

FRENCH FRIES

It was February when Diane suggested that I stop performing.
I did, but by June, I was second-guessing my decision. I was bored
and sad and would get insanely jealous when I'd see photos online
of other bands playing at places that I had performed the year prior.
James was now three and still not walking, which meant lots of lifting
on my end. I found myself lying on icepacks every night trying to fix
the problem.

One time he sat on my lap. Most mothers would think this was
an awesome thing, but I knew what it meant. I knew he was sick. The
only time he would let me hold him was when he was sick. So, one
Saturday we both lay on the couch and watched *Finding Nemo* for the
umpteenth time. But as many times as it had been on, I had never
watched it all the way through. Not wanting to disturb James, I kept
watching.

In case you haven't seen it, a clownfish named Marlin lives in the Great Barrier Reef with his son Nemo. One day, Nemo is abducted by a diver. Marlin sets out to find Nemo when he meets Dory, a blue tang fish suffering from short-term memory loss. Together, Marlin and Dory encounter all kinds of trials as they travel. At one point they are lost in the ocean and Dory resolves to ask a minke whale for directions. She starts speaking "whale", asking for help, and then the whale pulls them into his mouth. Trapped, Marlin tries to break out, sure they are going to die. Dory tries to console him as the whale emits a call and the water in the mouth begins to drain. Dory shouts, "He is saying that it's time for us to let go. Everything is gonna be alright."

But Marlin refuses to believe her. "You can't speak whale! How do you know? How do you know something bad isn't going to happen?" he begs.

And with that Dory says, "I don't," and they let go.

I gasped out loud. "What? Wait! You can't just let go! You're going to be swallowed alive! Oh, this is bad, this is really bad." And then, as you probably expected, the coolest thing happens. They fall to the back of the throat where they get shot out of the whale's blowhole.

I sat in disbelief. How did I not see that coming? They were safe, and able to continue on their journey and all they had to do was let go.

My tears dropped onto James' cheeks. I so badly wanted a guarantee that everything was going to be okay. I knew I wanted to let go, but I couldn't release my grip. I was hanging on to my fear, thinking it was protecting me and in truth, it was just keeping me stuck.

My sessions with Diane seemed to get worse instead of better. And it hurt like hell. When people tell me they've gone to therapy once or twice and now they are better, it makes me smile.

Because seeing a therapist is like dating. The first couple of weeks there's a lot of wooing and trying to impress. It's not until a few weeks in that you're ready to talk about your mother.

At about six to eight weeks in you start to touch on the important things, and the scab that covers up whatever wound you don't want to feel or see, starts to get picked at and then it starts to bleed and it hurts. And you think, "Hey, I don't like that. I want another Band-Aid!" And you'll either let the scab fall off and start to clean out the wound and stay in therapy for another three months, or you won't.

In one session with Diane she asked me why I was so angry. I told her I was tired of people calling and emailing, saying things they probably read in a Hallmark card. "God only gives special kids to special parents. And Lynn, just remember God would never give you more than you can handle." I said, "Well, He has definitely overestimated my capabilities on this one because I'm clearly not handling this very well." All I really wanted to hear was someone say they couldn't possibly begin to understand how I felt. That they had no clue about what I was going through. That's it. I try to remember this when I am with a friend who is hurting.

Occasionally I found myself wanting to punch people. I got a letter in the mail from a former "Christian friend" who assured me that James had Down syndrome and I was depressed because I had backslidden. And one time I was at Gymboree buying James some new clothes. He sat in his stroller playing with the sock monkey my sister had made him out of my father's socks. A woman approached me and said, "He is so cute!" Which of course made me start to cry. To console me she added, "Oh honey, it's okay. There's a sweet Downs boy who bags my groceries." What I was thinking was, "Thank you for that optimistic view of my son's future, but I had bigger dreams for him than bagging your fucking groceries." Of course, I didn't say anything out loud. I smiled, left and went to McDonald's.

Thankfully, I've never tried heroin. And I won't, because I'm sure heroin and I would become best friends. I've heard my brother Lud talk about the high he used to get and I get tingly just listening. Diane asked me once, "So, what do you do when you're feeling tense?"

~

My mom stood at the living room window, half-way hiding behind the heavy black and white brocade curtain, watching. And as soon as she saw my dad's red Lincoln Continental coming down the street, she put a twenty-dollar bill in my hand and sent me off down the street the other way, to McDonald's—a perfectly orchestrated dance.

As soon as I passed the white stone bench at the end of the driveway and made it to the front of my friend Jennifer Polz's house, I felt the release. The pressure to perform, to be quiet, to not say the wrong thing—was gone. Reaching the empty field behind Mike & Reggie's Beverage store, I skipped as the aroma of French fries filled the air. My heart was lifted and I felt peace.

An orange pop, large fry and plain hamburger was always my order. I knew all the teenagers that worked behind the counter. And they knew me. I was there a lot. I stuffed a wad of change into the front pocket of my jean shorts. I sat on the white and red tiled bench at the side of the building and ate, as slowly as I could.

When I finished, I headed to Mapletown. First to the Rite Aid where I would read the newest *Teen Beat*, then to the movie theater to see if there was a new poster in the glass case that sat outside. I'd walk all the way down to Aleschi's Grocer just to smell the Italian sausage and homemade bread. Then, I crossed back over Broadway, the busy four-lane street, and headed back up Stanley Avenue. By the time I reached the Polz's front yard, I could see if it was there or not. The driveway was empty. I could go home.

~

After leaving Diane's office, I picked James up from the nanny's and we headed to McDonald's. I knew I had sucked James into my own craziness when the window attendant saw him in the back seat and said, "Hey James, how ya doing?" And, like always, the calming factor was immediate.

I ate most of the fries and handed a few back to James. Jim borrowed my car later that day. He came home and said, "Lynn, why are there are French fries in our air vents?"

"I put them in there to cool them off before I hand them back to James," I said. Another reason I wasn't going to win "Mother of the Year".

I was now part of this new club, "The Down Syndrome Mothers of America." Did I mention I hate clubs? And there were all these new rules I was learning. Some of them were good, like the correct language to use. For instance, it's Down syndrome—capital "D" small "s". And don't ever use the slang and say, "Oh, bless her heart she has a Downs baby." I also learned about the order of words: people first, illness second. So you should say, "She has a baby with Down syndrome." And you should never say, "Oh, their baby isn't normal." The word normal should be replaced by the word typical. Because who's to say what is normal? There's an uncle on my mom's side who has all the right number of chromosomes and I can tell you for sure he ain't right. So the word to use is typical. And lastly, I learned the "R" word is off limits forever and ever, amen.

But following these rules and wearing a happy face when talking about James was hard for me. I was still not doing motherhood well. Mothers are supposed to be selfless. The kids are supposed to come first. But James didn't. I came first. And all I could think about was everything I didn't want.

But this is how the universe functions. Because I believe that our thoughts become things, focusing on my fear every day started to bring it closer to me. You know how when you start thinking about buying a new car, all of a sudden you see that make and model constantly? This is what happened to me. Jim and I would run into people with Down syndrome everywhere. One time, while on a beach in Naples, I was lying still, trying hard to not let my post-baby jiggles jiggle, and I heard Jim yelling from down the beach. "Lynn, Lynn, look who I just met!" It was a family of four with a boy with Down syndrome.

"Please forgive me if I don't sit up."

Jim was always great about approaching people, and learning all he could from their journey. Me, it just made me sad and crabby and more aware of my inability to cope. But one time I did try.

I was in Las Vegas helping to produce the Academy of Country Music Awards Red Carpet Show for the GAC (Great American Country) Network. After work one night I decided to head over to the Paris Las Vegas Hotel & Casino to get a crêpe.

As I stood under the miniature version of the Eiffel Tower, I noticed the family in front of me. It was easy to tell, even from behind. Her wide gait. Her larger hips. And the closer I got the better I could hear her awkward tongue. I wanted to run away, but something kept drawing me closer. I kept hearing Jim's voice in my head, "Go say hi to them, Lynn, they don't bite."

I had a chance to prove I could do this. I could be strong enough to face my fear of James being a teenager and say hello. I followed them into the casino and before I knew it I was on their heels, obviously close enough to make the dad feel uncomfortable. They stopped and he turned around and said, "Can I help you?"

I tried to speak. But I knew as soon as I opened my mouth the dam would break. I pointed to his daughter and mumbled, "I have one too," like she was a puppy or a toothache. Before I got to the end of the sentence, I was sobbing.

They smiled politely and walked away.

I collapsed in a slot machine chair.

I found my way to the crêpe place. I ordered a hot Nutella crêpe with vanilla ice cream. It looked pretty at first. But then the hot mixed with the cold and it turned into mush. This is how my insides felt. I wanted to be strong and able to confront my fear of Down syndrome, but I wasn't there yet. And I hated myself for what I really thought about that family. I hated that I thought they all looked tired and sad and frumpy. And I hated that I couldn't understand her speech. But mostly I hated the fact that this was going to be my future. My tears dropped onto the plate. I couldn't wait to get back home and into my robe.

But all my robe sitting and donut eating had taken its toll. Getting dressed one morning I realized that I had even grown out of my underwear. So I headed to T.J.Maxx to buy new ones when I passed Jim coming up the street. We stopped and rolled down our windows, but before I could speak he said, "Lynn, where's James?" Cue the *Home Alone* movie moment, because that's where James was. Home alone. I forgot I had him.

I turned the car around. James was safe, right where I left him, in his room playing with his sock monkey. I tried to hug him and tell him how sorry I was that I left him. But I knew he didn't understand. And that made me even sadder.

Jim was the strong one. The one who picked up my slack. The present one. But he had practice. His brother Kevin had Muscular Dystrophy and died at the age of sixteen. Jim knew what it was like live with a person with a disability. I was grateful for all he was doing but would never tell him. On the surface we looked fine. But our communication had dwindled down to necessity and in his silence I could still feel the anger. And now, it was a twenty-year-old wound.

~

Jim and I left San Diego and moved to Nashville in the mid-1990s. We loved the beach, and hated leaving it behind, but I was hoping a new city, a new house and new friends all might be good for our relationship. We also hoped that living in an entertainment town like Nashville might be good for our careers. I took a full-time job working as a producer for dick clark productions. I loved working in television, but I couldn't quit music.

In one of those fluke this-can't-be-happening-to-me events I got a message on my answering machine one day. "Hey Lynn, this is Chet—Chet Atkins. I heard that you play the accordion and I was wondering if you'd like to come down to Café Milano this Monday night and play a few tunes with me."

That evening will always be one of my most treasured career moments. After playing a few songs for a very enthusiastic crowd, Chet pulled me aside backstage. "Lynn, did you see how much the people enjoyed you? Why are you not playing polka for a living?"

I said, "You know, I'm not exactly sure the words polka and living should be in the same sentence."

We both laughed.

He went on to encourage me, to tell me that it didn't matter what I called it, but that the people needed to hear it and experience it. Chet may be the most gracious, kindest soul I've ever had the privilege of knowing. I played with Chet again in his hometown of Knoxville, Tennessee on June 12, 1998. It was his last public performance.

I took Chet's advice and made the decision to go into the studio and record. But I needed money. My mom's dad played a 1905 Mervar button accordion. And after his death, it was handed down to me. It had a very unique inset keyboard, which made it difficult for me to play. So it mostly sat on the shelf and collected dust. In what can only be described as one of my most stupid life choices, I sold it for $3,000.

I guess in the end there was some good that came out of selling the accordion. That $3,000 enabled me to record the *One Look* CD, and a song called "That's What I Like About The North" which became the most requested song on the morning shows of several country radio stations in the Midwest. And it all started because I dressed up as a can of Spam for Halloween, clearly showing how two completely unrelated events in your life might one day make sense.

While working on *Prime Time Country* on The Nashville Network, my friend Laurens and I decided to dress up for Halloween. Laurens (named after the city Laurens, South Carolina) is beautiful and blonde and a vegetarian. She is the sole reason that there is even a trace of vegetables in my diet today. And she's the most creative person I know.

With large boxes, construction paper, glue and a Sharpie, she made Spam can costumes mimicking the dancing cigarette boxes of the 1950s television commercials, complete with hats made of tin foil.

We appeared on the show with country music artists Trace Adkins, The Oak Ridge Boys and Little Jimmy Dickens. The next day, the morning show team of Jim Mantel and John Dobeck of WGAR Radio in Cleveland were talking about it and my sister Karie, a huge country music fan, was listening. She called in to the radio station and said, "Hey, that's my sister you're talking about! She was one of the dancing cans of Spam." A few minutes later my phone rang in Nashville. "Hey, is this Lynn? You are live on the air on WGAR in Cleveland. Are you one of the dancing cans of Spam?"

Being a dancing can of Spam started a relationship with Jim and John and when the *One Look* CD was released a few months later, they agreed to have me on as a guest, mostly to talk more about working with country music artists. But when I played "That's What I Like About The  North" live that morning, the phones lit up. Their listeners loved it and soon it became the most requested song in the history of the morning show. Before I knew it, I was a guest on morning radio shows in cities all across the northern US, including Chicago and Philadelphia and Milwaukee, all with the same results. It was a huge shot in the arm for my polka career. And I started performing more than ever.

One time, I did a gig in Helena, Montana. I was standing at the bar after my show when an elderly gentleman approached me. He said, "LynnMarie, you don't know me but my name is Bud Butterfield. My wife and I would like to invite you over to our house for some chili." A starving artist will never turn down a free home-cooked meal.

I sat and ate and enjoyed our conversation. Then he said, "I think I have something you're gonna want to see." I followed him down the stairs into his basement. And there, on a shelf, sat my grandfather's accordion. Bud Butterfield collected Mervar Accordions, and there in his basement in Montana were dozens of them, including my grandfather's. He lifted it off the shelf and placed it in my hands. The beauty in the moment was mixed with the mean voices in my head telling me how stupid I was to sell such a rare and special piece of my family story.

It was close to a decade later when I was playing a gig in Pennsylvania and a woman approached me. "Lynn, I'm not sure if you remember me or not but you came to my house once in Montana for chili. I am Bud Butterfield's wife." Before I could answer she handed me an envelope. "Bud passed away a few months ago. He spent his life admiring and caring for his accordion collection, but in

My Grandfather & his Mervar, circa 1962

his death he wanted each one of the instruments to go back to their original owners. The accordion will be back in your arms within the next month." I knew that this was bigger than me. I was acutely aware of and so grateful for God's grace. Grace is the English translation of the Greek word, *charis*— that which brings delight, joy, happiness, or good fortune.

Sometimes God's grace is so tangible you can squeeze it.

God does care about our broken hearts and our troubled minds, and, lucky for me, even our accordions.

"Not until we are lost do we begin to understand ourselves."
~ Henry David Thoreau ~

7.

JIM

I had been at ORU for a little over two months and I embraced all I was being taught. Rarely questioning anything. The advice of my brother, teachers, and my new friends on how I should live and act and believe were all I had to hang onto. Without them, I would most likely fall back into the deep dark hole of despair I had been in just a few months prior. Now, because I knew Jesus and was filled with the Holy Spirit I was full of joy. At least that's what they said. In hindsight, if Larry would have converted to Judaism, or become a Mormon, I could be celebrating Hanukkah or living in Utah right now. I was in pain; he provided relief. It was that simple.

But by November the pain was back. Because nothing was really fixed. And something inside started saying, "Hey wait, your dad is still an alcoholic and your mom is still dead! What about all that?" When I would bring this to anyone's attention, they would quote 2

Corinthians 5:17: "This means that anyone who belongs to Christ has become a new person. The old life is gone; a new life has begun!" (NLT) I hated this answer and still do. It seems to be the fall back for many church counselors and it just doesn't work for me.

Loving Jesus is true and real. But so is dysfunction and disease.

You can move, change your surroundings, break up with a boy, even say all the right things, but if you're not dealing with the real issues, you'll just end up back where you started. Or worse, more lost. Being quoted scripture by my new friends who were mostly raised in Christian homes didn't help. I was secretly contemplating leaving ORU, but then I met Jim.

My desire to play my accordion still lingered deep inside. Even though it was in the closet, I still longed for its comfort. I thought I could justify playing it, if I found a university-sanctioned mission trip that was even remotely European and used it to play Christian music. I walked around the Missions Conference held on campus, looking for a place that might embrace my music. The closest I could get to my roots was Finland. Nowhere near Slovenia, but at least on the same continent. I spoke with the team leader, Pete, who introduced me to Jim Rink. He had traveled to Finland the year before and would be willing to tell me about his trip. We spoke for a few minutes. I told him about my accordion. He seemed both intrigued and unsure. Then he took my hands and asked if he could pray with me. At this time in my life, this was the sexiest thing a guy could have done. The code of conduct that you had to sign when being accepted to ORU stated, "I will not partake in any public display of affection," along with the unspoken pressure that you would have minimal, if not any, sexual contact with the opposite sex until you were married. Jim and I finished praying and I walked into the chapel. The same chapel I had sat in just a few months prior.

As I walked down the aisle, I swear I heard a voice in my head say, "You're going to marry him." Today, I'm not sure if I really heard it or not. I don't know if it was spiritual peer pressure; all of my friends were always hearing things from God. Or maybe God truly did speak to my spirit that day. The only thing I do know is that believing I heard God enabled me to survive the rocky courtship ahead. I was undeterred, because I believed in my heart we were going to be together.

And so we were. A year later we got engaged and the following June we got married. We ignored all the red flags, mostly because we didn't see them at the time.

We were living our perfect lives. We had perfect Christian friends. We listened to only Christian music. We worked in Christian television for Oral and Richard Roberts on their daily national television show. Then we moved to San Diego and worked for a television ministry there as well.

But three years into the marriage, things weren't as they appeared. Jim and I had each brought our own baggage to the relationship, but we were too young to even realize we had baggage. We were taught to believe  that marriage was supposed to be easy because of Jesus. Sex was supposed to be great because we waited. But now, it was frustrating and we were growing apart.

When I met and married Jim, I morphed into Jim. I became who he needed, who he wanted. I dressed the way he suggested, I worked where he suggested. He couldn't have known then that his suggestions were killing me. That by making decisions for me, he was picking up where my brother Larry had left off, and before him, where my mom had left off. Nobody knew this was the worst thing they could do for me. They just thought they were helping. But I took their words and made a life out of them.

I followed Jim around like a wet puppy and had no sense of direction for my own life.

Occasionally my dad would call with the usual questions like, "When are you kids going to get real jobs?" and "Why haven't you called your sister Karie?" But one day, he called and didn't drill me. Instead he said, "Hey, I'm going to Europe on a two-week tour to meet our relatives, and I'd like to know if you want to go with me?" I was ecstatic. The idea of traveling around Europe for two weeks sounded awesome. (I never did end up going to Finland on that mission trip because I couldn't raise enough financial support.) So here was my chance to finally travel overseas. But then he said, "I'll take you with me, but you've got to do something for me." I knew it. There was a catch. There was always a catch.

He said, "You have to bring you accordion."

It was as if those words came directly out of the devil's mouth. I hoped he was kidding and I wanted to remind him that playing in a non-Christian environment–would surely screw up my eternal life. But he insisted and I didn't resist. I pulled the accordion out from the back of the closet and hoped it would still play.

I don't believe my dad knew the weight of what he was asking. He just missed seeing his little girl play. And neither one of us knew the enormity of what was about to happen.

But desire, when paired with God's plan, can change the course of a life.

Crossing the border from Austria into Slovenia felt like walking into the doors at The Nash. I was home. The rolling hills and the Catholic steeples seemed so familiar and yet it was my first visit. The Slovenian language I learned as a child made me feel a part of this place. Like my soul had already been there. That evening, the bandleader hosting the trip, Joey Tomsick, asked me to join them on stage.

This was the first time I'd be on this kind of stage since I'd become a Christian. My heart raced as I stepped onto the platform. I strapped on my accordion and Joey shortened the microphone to my height. He counted the song off, "One, two, three, four," and as I pushed down on the buttons, and something as powerful as that moment in the ORU chapel happened to me. There, surrounded by what I was taught to believe was bad—drinking, smoking and the hell-bound Catholics—I felt alive. Fully alive. I felt more alive than any bible verse or devotional had made me feel. I felt more alive than being in church or in an ORU Chapel service. I felt happy and joyful and complete. It was a high like I hadn't felt in years.

For the entire vacation I partied and laughed and played. I played on the street corner in Munich and on the eight-hour bus ride from Switzerland to Slovenia. I played at the pig roast my family gave to welcome us. I drank homemade whiskey and got tipsy for the first time since Bowling Green. But this time it wasn't because I wanted to *not* feel, it was because I wanted *to* feel. It wasn't about hiding, but about feeling alive. It was about breaking the rules. And part of me was so happy.

But I had been taught (and some might say brainwashed) to believe this would surely be the way the devil would arrive. He would use what I loved most to pull me back into the darkness. So, at the end of each day, alone in my room, I'd fall onto my knees and beg God to forgive me and not send me to hell.

Within days after my return I told Jim I wasn't sure about God, him, or marriage. And not long after that was when I thought about driving my car off the cliff and when I met Bob.

Bob recommended a lot of books, all with the word codependent in the title. In one book, *Codependent No More* by Melody Beattie, I read, "Feel what you feel and know what you know". This was such a simple statement and yet so foreign to me. I had no idea I was allowed to have my own feelings, let alone trust them. At the same time, Jim recommended a really small book called *The Subtle Power of Spiritual Abuse* by David Johnson and Jeff VanVonderen. Everything I read rang true for me. "Spiritual abuse is the result of a spiritual leader or system that tries to control, manipulate, or dominate a person. This control is often in the form of fear. They turn your view of God into one where He is seen as a harsh taskmaster, eagerly waiting for you to mess up so He can chastise you or leave you behind." I started to understand how damaging the church could be and how messed up some of its teachings were. I learned to separate the church and God. And learned the enormity of the difference. It would take me months, but I finally made sense of my love for the music and what I thought God thought about polka. I am happy to announce to the world that God loves polka! At least I think that's what She said.

But the process of developing a sense of self was only part of the challenge. The other rub was that in choosing to begin that journey, I was pulling further and further away from Jim, even though he was more supportive and more liberal than most born again Christians. But there was still a gap between us. I was trying to figure out what "I" thought about everything. And he got hurt and frustrated and angry.

So, in order to avoid conflict, I stopped sharing what I thought about anything, especially if I knew it went against Jim's desires and beliefs. What should have been a celebrated time of self-discovery ended up being something I had to do in secret. At the end of the day, I was still being codependent.

I had been in therapy with Bob for several weeks when he suggested it was time for Jim to join in. Jim willingly agreed. "It's because of your family that our marriage is a mess, so yes, I'll go so you can figure it out."

In that first session, Jim boldly told Bob, "Her family is a mess. It's full of drug addicts and alcoholics. I didn't come from a family like that. We don't have those kinds of problems." And I agreed with Jim. They were the perfect ones. They worked at the church. His father was an elder and his mom was the pastor's secretary for twenty-five years. They hugged each other daily and said "I love you" a lot. They had morning devotionals. Even though Kevin died, they all handled it perfectly because they knew Jesus. I believed at the time that I was absolutely the one who was screwed up and was screwing up. I was the sinner. And it seemed to be more about who I was, than what I was doing. It was as if because of my upbringing, I didn't measure up.

During one of our silent drives home after counseling, Jim and I started arguing about my desire to go back to Cleveland to play my accordion. Then he said, "Fine, if you want to do that, then you do not want to be a Rink." The words cut through me. I felt scared and lonely and unwanted. I was confused, because I truly did love Jim and parts of our life. But there was this deep, inner nagging to find my truth. I left everything I had known to be with Jim: my family, my father, and my culture. I needed to pay attention to the desire to have those things back in my life, even at the risk of losing Jim. It was a really hard time. And I didn't know how it was going to end up.

I told Bob that I didn't really have a choice and I felt stuck. I told him I had said "I do" for life and divorce wasn't an option.

Then he said, "Look, I'm not going to tell you whether you should stay with Jim or not, but I am going to tell you that after six months in therapy you'll be able to make a better decision."

Jim and I muddled through the next couple of months. It was awkward and hard. We were both still working for the ministry, but my heart was no longer in it. I wanted to quit, but that would make me even more of a sinner. I was so torn. And then one day, I wasn't.

The evangelist that we, and my brother Larry, were working for, whom I'll call Bill, was holding a big healing conference. I was working in the television truck as the assistant director and Jim was on stage working as a stage manager. The arena was packed with thousands of people and at the end of the service many came forward so Bill could lay his hands on them. At one point during that healing line, Bill held up his hands and announced to the crowd, "The anointing of God is on me. He has turned my hands red with fire and healing power."

Jim and I were in direct communication with each other over the headset. When Bill was finished, he headed backstage, with Jim right by his side. I heard Jim over the headset say, "Hey, we need to get Marcy (the make-up artist) back here—Bill's got something on his hands that needs to be wiped off." I asked Jim what he thought it was. He replied, "Marcy thinks it's hair dye."

A week later, while reviewing the video tapes from that evening, it was evident that it was in fact hair dye. But that didn't stop Bill from using this situation as a campaign to collect money from his followers. Everything inside me knew this was wrong and dishonest. But it was just what I needed.

For me, it was the push that helped me make my move. I may not have known exactly what I believed spiritually at the time, but I knew I didn't believe in what was going on around me. I was craving and longing for something real and this wasn't it.

A few days later I was trying to get dressed for work. I couldn't decide what to wear. I stared at two outfits on the bed. One Jim would like, one I liked. But I couldn't choose. I started crying and then the cries turned into weeping, and then I started banging my head against the wall until I bled. To someone else, it was a simple decision on what to wear to work. To me, it was the realization that I had no sense of self. I had no ability to make decisions for myself. I didn't know who I was and I clearly didn't know who God was.

I ran into Larry in the stairwell at work. He asked me how I was doing. I told him I had to leave. I told him that I was turning in my resignation and I could no longer work at a place where I didn't support the vision. He said, "Lynn, I think this is an issue with your faith. Are you having your devotionals? Are you spending time in prayer? Have you fasted?" I could feel the pull. I could hear the mean voices telling me I wasn't good enough. That I was a sinner. That I was disobeying God's will. That I didn't know what I was talking about. That my daddy wasn't drunk even though I knew he was. But something shifted that day. It was so small; I can hardly believe it mattered. But I found the strength to make a choice.

It only takes moving a plane's navigational joystick a fraction of an inch to change its entire course.

"When someone you love dies, you don't lose her all at once;
you lose her in pieces over a long time — the way the mail
stops coming, and her scent fades from the pillows."
~ John Irving, A Prayer for Owen Meany ~

8.

BREASTS

Being the youngest of six was not easy. I got picked on a lot. And of course I was spoiled. I was a huge ball of energy, constantly moving, loud and obnoxious, starved for attention. I'm sure my siblings were angry because I got the attention they didn't. And whenever they could, they would take it out on me. Larry and Lenny would each take an arm, pin me down, and tickle me until I cried. They would offer me a quarter for every five minutes I would go into the other room and be quiet. But nothing they did has left such a scar on me as my memories of Christmas mornings.

~

The stairs, covered in worn green carpet, creaked as I slowly descended down. I held tightly to the wobbly wooden handrail, its bolts pulling away from the wall. I should have been excited to see what Santa had left me. It was one of the few times I didn't bounce down the stairs. I was only three and a half and filled to the brim with fear. Afraid, because I had been told by my brothers for weeks leading up to this day that I was not a good girl and Santa was going to leave me nothing but a big stick and coal and rocks.

My feet hit the bottom of the steps and I paused to straighten out the heel of my pale pink sock. I was the first one awake. It was silent, and as I turned the corner into the living room the shock was deafening. A five-foot wooden stick protruded out of my stocking. Santa's disapproval of my behavior, boldly displayed to provide a moment of public humiliation. I ran back upstairs as fast as I could. I fought back the tears as I huddled under my ballerina comforter. "Maybe I can pretend I didn't see it and when I go back down in a little bit it will be gone," I prayed.

I stayed in bed as long as I could. Torn between wanting to open presents but terrified to see The Stick. The next time down the steps I was met with laughter and taunting. My siblings made me pour the contents of the stocking out onto the floor like a game of show and tell. "Come on Lynn, what else did Santa bring you? Let's see it!" A rock, a piece of coal and a bar of soap.

But this wasn't just about a stick. It was about laying a foundation for feeling innately flawed. That no matter how hard I tried to be good, nothing I did would ever be good enough. Children are supposed to be built up and cared for, made to feel like they can do anything. I love the scene in the 2011 movie *The Help* when Abilene Clark says to the little girl, "You is kind. You is smart. You is important." Instead, what I felt that morning was that I was broken. And it was the birth of the shame I would carry for the next forty years.

The stick gag happened for about three years straight. And as horrible as it was, at the same time it made me feel loved. I mean, they were at least paying attention to me, right? If I could learn to hide the tears and bury the pain and just soak in the attention part, then maybe this wasn't such a bad thing. But for the life of me I can't understand why my mother let them do this.

There were other humiliating Christmas morning moments. Like the time when I was twelve and after opening all the presents my mom said, "Wait, there's one more present that she hasn't opened." Everyone began searching, going through trash bags of wrinkled paper and bows. I was filled with excitement wondering what it could be. My dad asked, "What the hell are we looking for, Lillian?"

"Her first bra."

I wanted to die. We never spoke about any body parts, especially breasts.

We never found it, and as humiliating as the process was, I sure wished we would have. I'd have to wait another six months to get a

hand-me-down one from the daughter of a family friend. And the fact I needed one was a bit of confirmation that playing the accordion was not a horrible mistake.

My first band was made up of my four cousins,

The Wolf Family Band, circa 1978

Johnny, Billy, Timmy and Ronnie and their best friend, Tom. We were the Wolf Family Band.

We grew up together, on the stages of county fairs, on the local *Polka Varieties* television show and riding in a van to and from gigs. We had band practice every Tuesday night in their basement. The walls were covered in a dark wood paneling, and without fail, every time I entered the room one of the boys would bang their hands against the wall and say, "Hey, is that you Lynn? I couldn't tell." Inferring that my chest was so flat they couldn't tell the difference between the wall and me. I was told that my breasts were never going to grow because I was always carrying around the box. No breasts *and* she plays the accordion. I didn't have a prayer.

But something happened behind that accordion. I could hide, not just my budding breasts, but also my sadness, my anger, my fear. I smiled on the outside as the shame took root on the inside. On that very first day when my dad secured the straps behind me, and we stared into each other's eyes, he said to me, "LynnMarie, no matter what happens in life, you just keep smiling." I intended to do just that.

~

I was surprised to see her in line at the ice cream stand where I was working between my junior and senior year of high school. It was the middle of July, extremely hot, and my mom hardly ever left the comfort of the air-conditioned house. She leaned down and spoke softly through the mesh screen, "Hey Kid," she said, "Can I get a chocolate shake and can you come out for a second?" From the tone of her voice I knew something wasn't right. I met her at the red painted picnic table. She was visibly shaking. I can't remember if I asked what was wrong or if she just said it. "They found a lump", she muttered. She hung her head and seemed embarrassed to be talking about her breast. We didn't talk about anything much in our house, let alone body parts, let alone ones that might be considered sexual. I felt like anything I said at that moment would sound empty or cliché. I managed to do both. "It'll be okay."

The lines grew outside the window and I was glad to have a reason to get back to work. I watched as she sat and sipped her shake and was relieved when she finally left.

The next couple of months were a flurry of doctor's visits, get well wishes and gift food. The fridge was always filled with tin foil-covered casseroles with a description and date written on a piece of masking tape. It's funny, because I don't remember eating any of it.

A radical left mastectomy. The doctors said they thought they got it all.

One Wednesday evening in October I came home from theater rehearsal. My father was walking from the kitchen to the living room where he'd just hung up the phone. He was angry. He looked at me and said, "Go pack your mother a bag. I'm taking her back to the hospital." I remember thinking that I wasn't sure who he was mad at—the person he just hung up the phone with, my mother for having to go back to the hospital, or me.

I walked into my mother's bedroom and I felt completely lost. She was the one who always took care of me. I had no idea how to take of her. I grabbed a small green suitcase from her closet and threw in a pair of pajamas. "Would she need underwear?" I thought, embarrassed to pick them up. I couldn't figure out what else to include. What would she need for yet another hospital stay? Should I pack clothes for her to come home? But something inside knew she wouldn't need them.

I handed my father the half-empty suitcase and he asked, "Did you pack her prosthetic?" Honestly, I swear I wasn't even sure I knew she had one. I mean, of course I did, they had removed her left breast four weeks prior. But he was now asking me to acknowledge that fact. I walked back into their bedroom and there on her nightstand was a bra, bigger than I imagined, with one side empty and one side filled with foam. I struggled to pick it up. Like holding it was the last straw in admitting my mother had breast cancer. I grabbed it and quickly shoved it into the outside pocket of the suitcase, scraping my hand on the zipper.

I watched my father guide her down the steps and to the car. Her mid-section had blown up, like she was nine months pregnant. With his hand on her arm, he didn't seem mad anymore. As he loaded her in the car, he looked at me, and in an empty tone, one I had never heard before, he said, "LynnMarie, tell your mother you love her."

"It'll be okay," I mumbled.

I sat at the kitchen table, in my mother's favorite chair, and watched the taillights fade as they drove down the street. But before they disappeared around the bend, I screamed out at the top of my lungs, "Mom, I love you! I love you! I need you! Don't leave me!" And as I licked the blood from the scratch on the back of my hand, I knew my mother was never coming home.

She had been on a morphine drip for two weeks and the doctor said she wouldn't last but a couple days more. I hadn't been to see her much at all. Karie sat me down and said, "Lynn, you really need to go to the hospital." I hated everything about that hospital room. The lighting, the sounds and the pink swab they used to clean around her gums.

Auntie Olga and Mrs. Bergman were in the room when I arrived. It was quiet. My mom hadn't spoken in close to forty-eight hours. After a few minutes, I figured I had fulfilled my duty. When I went to say goodbye, I somehow found the strength to bend over and kiss her forehead. She already felt cold. I was almost to the door when I heard her mumble.

"What did she say?"

"Nothing, you go on," said Auntie Olga.

"No, what did she say?" I asked again. Back at her bedside I leaned in close. "Mom, did you want to tell me something?" I asked softly.

What seemed like minutes later, she breathed in deep and quietly said, "I can't love you anymore."

She died twenty-four hours later. Mrs. Bergman was in the room as my father hugged my mother as she took her final breath. Mrs.

Bergman said it was a cloudy October day, and yet on her white hospital sheet appeared a rainbow. A swath of color across her chest. And when she died, the rainbow slowly made its way to the end of the bed and disappeared.

~

I came in one afternoon from swimming in our backyard pool, to find my mother standing over the kitchen sink, sobbing. I asked her what was wrong. She tried to say it was just allergies and I pretended to believe her. It was the only time I ever saw her cry.

Lud & Sandy's Wedding, 1968

But she was so sad after Sandy, my brother Lud's wife, had passed away, that I'm surprised I didn't catch her crying more often.

Lud and Sandy were high school sweethearts. They survived a near-death car accident together at eighteen. And they had been married for eight years when she went in for a routine surgery to untangle the nerves at the base of her brain. But nothing about the surgery or the days that followed was routine.

Sandy slipped into a coma. A nurse slipped my brother a note saying that he should investigate the doctor. There were rumblings of the wrong kind of anesthesia and too much of it. It's going to make a great *Forensic Files* episode one day. Larry flew in. The house was full of visitors and gift food.

After twelve days in a coma, the doctors convinced my brother Lud to leave the hospital, and Sandy's side, for the first time. He did. Then, at 2 a.m., Lenny, Larry and Lud, all in different houses, were each strangely awoken by a feeling. They all three separately headed to the hospital. When they got there, they were told that

Sandy had just died. It didn't take long for Lud to begin covering his pain with heroin.

Sandy's death was a shock but death was not unfamiliar. My mom's parents had died just about a year earlier. My grandpa died first, then six weeks later, my grandma. They had been married over fifty years. They said my grandma died of a broken heart.

After my grandparents died, my mom ended up in an argument, and then a full-blown legal dispute, over their estate with her one and only sister, Mitzi. They were best friends up until the day I found my mom crying over the sink. My mom had to call the police and have Mitzi removed from our house. They didn't speak for the last seven years my mom was alive. Mitzi showed up at my mom's side when she was on her deathbed, begging for forgiveness.

So, by the time she got cancer, I think my mom was just tired. In one year she had lost four of the people closest to her. And she was tired of trying to keep the dysfunction functioning. For years I was angry with her for what I thought was her unwillingness to fight; for being weak. But I understand her more today. She had an out, and she took it.

But what she left behind was a huge, gaping hole. The absence of her made everything that she took care of and handled extremely obvious. I was forced for the first time to try to make decisions for myself. But I had no skills to do that. It would be way easier to let my brother Larry take over where my mom left off.

Mom, Sandy & Me, 1977

~

As I sat at the sticky picnic table at Bobby's Dairy Dip in Nashville and watched James eat his fries, I realized how much I still missed her. I longed to feel her tough love. Even though a part of me knew she most likely would be mad at me. Disappointed in me for being so weak. She had this "quit complaining and just do it" mentality. I imagine that had she lived she would have been the one to constantly be telling me to get over myself.

But had she lived, my life would have taken me down different roads. It would have been her voice that sent me to the Academy of Dramatic Arts in New York, but then I may not have ever reached the bottom and the need to reach out to God. The loss of her made room for more life.

<blockquote>
The one thing I know to be true about the death of anything, is it always makes room for something new.
</blockquote>

> *"If a problem is fixable, if a situation is such that you can do something about it, then there is no need to worry. If it's not fixable, then there is no help in worrying. There is no benefit in worrying whatsoever."*
> ~ *Dalai Lama* ~

9.

FIXABLE

The first time I knew something was wrong I was sitting in a dark control room. I was working on a program for the Christian Broadcasting Network called *Turning Point*. As I listened to the host use words like healing and grace and faith, I knew the baby inside of me was not okay. I tried to focus on the stopwatches in front of me, but with every second that clicked by, the cramping got stronger and harder to ignore. Then I started spotting. I knew exactly what was happening. I'd been through this before, with my first miscarriage, during my debut appearance on the Grand Ole Opry, and then again with my second miscarriage a few years later. So I assumed I knew what was coming next.

This baby would die too.

I was leaving the production facility when the make-up artist stopped me. She asked if I was okay and even though I barely knew her, I told her I knew there was a problem with my pregnancy. She told me that she believed it was going to be okay and that she would pray for me. I wanted to ask her nicely not to. I wanted to tell her that I didn't believe much in prayer anymore and wasn't even sure what I believed about God. I wanted to say that I thought all these born again evangelical Christians were full of shit, even though I used to be one of them, and that if one more person called to tell me I was being put on a prayer chain I might just go postal. And another thing, if it is true, what the host said today, that everything is God's will, why even pray? What is prayer going to do if losing this baby is part of God's plan? Would God change his mind if the number of prayer warriors got high enough? Does God think, "Oh wait, maybe I'll change the plan because now the pastor of the largest church in Dallas is praying."

But I didn't say any of those things. I smiled and thanked her and left.

It wouldn't be until years later when I would come to believe this:

Prayer is not about changing a situation; it's about changing my own heart and mind to see the beauty in what isn't budging.

Sometimes all the prayer in the world won't change things. Sometimes things are just not fixable.

~

Getting the first Grammy nomination in 2001 was such an exciting time. If you would have been watching from the outside, you would have thought I had been nominated for "Best New

Artist" or "Song of the Year", not "Best Polka Album". Needless to say, we took advantage of the experience 110%.

Part of that involved getting a designer to make a dress for me for the red carpet. A friend suggested a "friend of a friend" who was graduating from a design school in Chicago. She emailed me a few of her designs and I picked the perfect one — a beautiful ice blue satin dress with a high collar and plunging V neckline, almost down to my belly button. It had strands of crystal beads that would drape across my chest, holding together just enough material to cover my breasts.

I sent measurements to Chicago and as the Grammys neared I flew up for my final fitting. When I slipped it on I saw multiple issues, but I knew the dress wasn't finished so I didn't fret too much about what I saw. She had a few more days to finish it, and then she would mail it to our hotel in Los Angeles.

The dress arrived in a FedEx package to my hotel room the day before the Grammys. My niece Katey and my friend Dottie were in the room with me when I put it on. What I saw on their faces said it all. The dress looked almost exactly as it did at the last fitting. It looked like a sixth grader had sewn it. Nothing was even, and when I tried to make the collar even on top, my left boob would fall out of the dress. Katey, who doesn't filter her words said, "Aunt Lynn, you can not wear that dress."

Jim has an amazing ability to be calm in the midst of chaos, so he picked up the phone and called the concierge. Within minutes the hotel seamstress was knocking at the door. Jim said, "Let's see if she can fix this."

I answered the door to find Maria, a lovely Mexican woman who was just about as wide as she was tall. (If you've ever stayed at the Biltmore Hotel in downtown L.A. you would know why I was concerned about her width. Our extremely tiny room barely had room for us, let alone the addition of Maria.)

As we squeezed into the only open floor space available, Maria took one look at the dress and quickly said, "Oh problemo!"

I said, "Yeah, there's a problem!"

Over and over Maria kept saying, "Oh problemo! Oh problemo! Oh problemo!" And then seeing my impending meltdown she added, "I FIX! I FIX! You no a worry. I fix!"

In the five minutes it took for Maria to get to our room I did some close examination of the dress and realized if we could make one of the strands of beads a little tighter, it might hold it all together enough so I wasn't having a wardrobe malfunction on the red carpet. The dress had a total of fourteen fake crystal beads on one strand and I thought if we took out five and made it nine, it would help tremendously. So I told Maria I wanted there to only be nine beads and her response was, "Oh problemo. I fix." Soon, after enough repetition, she added nueve to her list of words. "Oh problem, I fix, nueve."

Jim jumped in and asked in broken English, "Maria, yes you fix, but you think fixable?" Her response, "Oh problemo. I fix. Nueve." It was at this point that I realized she didn't speak English.

As I handed the dress over to Maria I started sobbing. Jim looked at his watch and said, "Lynn, you have two hours to get to the Beverly Center, buy a backup dress, and get back here for tonight's party." Dottie volunteered to go with me.

Dottie and I have known each other since 1996, when we both worked for dick clark productions on *Prime Time Country*. We became friends in the midst of producing chaotic television segments that involved country music artists, flying chickens and inflated egos. So Dottie and I, and my friends Laurens and Stacey Jo, became like one big support group. They say siblings in dysfunctional families share a tight bond especially when raised around any kind of abuse. So is the case with co-workers.

When the show ended in 1999, Dottie and I entered the television freelance market together. I used to tell people that I may have been the reason we got called for the job (being a bit outspoken) but Dottie was definitely the reason we kept the job! She is talented and Southern—which means she is much nicer than me. She has the ability to tell people to go to hell and they will look forward to the trip. She is also extremely organized which was why Jim hired her to help with the flurry of business that arrived because of the first Grammy nomination.

Dottie and I ran through the Beverly Center, looking like rats in a maze searching for cheese. Soon, I was out of time. In Bloomingdales, I picked out six dresses and didn't even have time to try any of them on. Dottie said to the saleswoman, "Look, I'm going to be honest with you, we will be bringing five of these dresses back." The woman nodded and rang up the over $3,000 bill.

I made it back to the room in time to change and get to the nomination reception. For that one night I was an equal to all other nominees. I took photos with people like Weird Al Yankovic and met Queen Latifah and Bruce Springsteen. My friend had a private party for us at his home in the Hollywood Hills. I felt like a rock star. Or at least a polka rock star.

It was well after midnight by the time we made it back to the Biltmore. The dress from Maria was hanging in the closet. About fifteen family members and friends all squeezed into the room to see the fixed dress. As I slipped it out of the clear plastic cover I could see there were in fact nine beads and I was so excited. Maybe she did understand after all. And maybe it was fixable. As the dress fell on my hips and down to the floor I looked up and once again saw the answer their faces. "Aunt Lynn, you can *not* wear that dress." It was not fixable.

I started trying on the six dresses I had bought at Bloomingdales. With everyone's help we settled on "the best" one. Not my dream dress, not the dress I planned on walking my first red carpet in, but one that would work. It was a satin fuchsia dress with spaghetti straps and with extra material that draped low in the front and very low in back.

Someone said, "Turn around so we can see the back." And as I did, there was a collective gasp. A group inhale that seemed to suck the air right out of the room.

"What?! What is wrong?" I asked.

My sister Karie was the first one to speak. "It's okay Lynn, take the dress off and give it to me. I will figure it out. Just give me the dress."

"What is wrong?" I asked again. I pushed my way to the mirror, and I saw it. Attached to the low-slung back, smack dab in the middle of my butt, was the white plastic security tag sensor. Apparently the sensor didn't go off when I left the store because there were so many dresses in the bag. At this point I had had about all the drama that even I could handle. I handed the dress to Karie. I knew she would make it work.

After a morning full of radio and television appearances and an 11 a.m. live appearance on CNN, I made it back to my room. Karie had just finished ironing the dress and I slipped it on. Only later would I hear the entire story. That the concierge herself drove the dress back to Bloomingdales to have the security tag removed, then, got it to Maria who hemmed it. The dress had arrived in my room just twenty minutes before I had to be on the red carpet.

The ice blue satin dress still hangs in my closet. I pull it out whenever I need reminded not to waste too much energy on things that are clearly not fixable.

The Grammys, 2001

~

As I drove home from the television studio I continued to struggle with God's will versus prayer. Why would I pray for God to change the situation if everything in the end is under His control? And why would I pray for Him to perform a miracle when I knew deep down my whole life that this was going to be my destiny?

The next morning I sat in Dr. Blake's office. She put the stethoscope on my belly and for the first time I heard the heartbeat. It was strong. I was shocked and perplexed. I didn't think the baby would still be alive. She sent me for an ultrasound.

As I lay on the ultrasound table, I could tell by the look on the face of the technician that she saw something disconcerting. She stayed in one spot way too long. Pushing down on the wand to get just the right picture. Jim stood nearby. Worried, but wearing his optimistic face. The technician went to get the doctor. I sat there in the blue backless paper dress and noticed my toenails needed to be painted.

The fetal specialist came into the room. I could tell by the non-expression on his face that bad news was coming and my first thought was, "This is hardly the attire I wish to be in for such a life-changing event. I would at least like my ass to be covered up."

In the most monotone, clinical and unemotional voice, the specialist said. "So, we think the baby you are carrying has what's called Turner syndrome. We won't know for sure until we can do an amniocentesis in a few weeks. But there is a fifty percent chance that you are having a girl and she

Žužemberk, 2005

has Turner syndrome. What this means is she will be short in stature, she will come out with webbed hands and feet, a webbed neck—all of which can be taken care of surgically. But she will be short, taller than a dwarf, but short. However, she will be mentally okay. Any questions?"

Yes, a million. But none I want to talk to you about. You are a cold mean bastard and I want you out of my face; no, actually I'd like to punch your face. You just described to me in thirty seconds that I am giving birth to a webbed human. He handed me a shiny, colorful brochure to take home with me.

Fully dressed and in the car, I sobbed all the way to the airport. Jim was leaving that afternoon for Europe, going ahead of me to prepare things for the following weeks' handful of shows I would have in Slovenia, and I couldn't wait to put him on that plane. He asked if I felt like he should stay behind, but I was secretly mad at him and glad he was leaving. Like somehow all this was his fault. That I should have listened to my gut and not had kids. And because I didn't listen and went with what was the expected, next, right thing to do in our twenty-year-plus marriage, we were now having a deformed baby. And if he was out of my sight, maybe I could somehow forget this was happening.

I met up with Jim in Slovenia a week later. The welcome reception my relatives and the town of Žužemberk threw for me was over the top, complete with traditional food, music and gifts, held in a thousand-year-old castle near the birthplace of my grandfather. I passed on the local wine, Cviček, knowing Jim would frown upon it, but what I was really thinking was, "What the fuck does it matter anyway? I'm having a webbed child; how much worse could a glass of wine make it?"

We hadn't planned on telling anyone in Slovenia we were having a baby, let alone a webbed one. We were in the midst of trying to get my career off the ground in that country, and I believed a baby was sure to kill it. But then, a cousin made a comment that I looked like I had put on a few pounds and I snapped. There was no way in hell I was going to be fat on top of all of this. "Guess what?" I said. "Ja sem noseča! I'm pregnant!" Happily they toasted, and convinced Jim that one glass of wine was good for the baby and for me. I gulped it down.

We celebrated Thanksgiving in Slovenia and as I bowed my head to pray, all I could think about was how much I wanted to die. I did not want to be here, there, anywhere. On the land where my blood came from, I couldn't help but wish I had never been born. That I would have never survived. I felt like I had nothing to offer the world, Jim, this baby. "Please God, what can I do to not feel this pain? Please don't make me do this!" Silence.

Throughout the trip and for the following month, the mantra I repeated over and over and over and over, even to the point of singing it at times was, "Turner syndrome is only a physical disease and her webbed hands, feet and neck would be fixable. Thank God it's not something horrible like Down syndrome!"

The amniocentesis was scheduled for the day after we returned from Europe. I watched on the monitor as the six-inch needle was inserted into my belly. I tried not to move or breathe, but part of me knew that if I did both, the baby would die. It would be an honest mistake. Somehow I stayed completely still. We'd have to wait another two weeks for the results.

"Chaos is a friend of mine."
~ Bob Dylan ~

10.

CHAOS

I had become really great at creating chaos. It seemed normal to me. The more the merrier, the more last minute the better, the more out of the box the better. It all made me feel more secure. I realized that this is part of my nature, because it is part of my family's nature; it got handed down like my mother's homemade bread recipe.

One time, this inherited DNA trait became crystal clear. We were a few hours away from having a large party at our house. There was still so much to do. KC came to town to help. If you are a crazy, self-indulged artist type, like me, then you absolutely need a KC in your life. The friend who is stable. Who remembers where the keys to the car are. Has extra batteries and gum in her purse. The friend who makes a to-do list and sticks to it. KC and I met on an elevator at a polka festival in Cleveland. We bonded instantly when we agreed that we were probably the only two twenty-six-year-olds who listened to polka music in their car. Plus, KC plays the button accordion, and her family is also from Slovenia, so we are kindred spirits.

It was early on in our friendship when we were filling each other in on our life stories when she said to me, "You know Lynn, this kind of stuff doesn't happen to everybody. You really need to write a book." And that was before depression and Down syndrome. Having KC as a friend is  like walking around with the person you wish you were. With her by my side she constantly challenges me to be better than I am.

KC is also an amazing cook and she was in the kitchen making the klobasi and pierogies for the party. I made a comment to Lenny that I wished I had had time to hang decorative lights on the patio. Thirty minutes later Lenny returned from Home Depot with a bucket, a bag of concrete and a twelve-foot 4x4. KC said, "Well of course we're mixing concrete and stringing patio lights thirty minutes before a party. This is what the Hrovats do!"

Thankfully, the lights got strung and they looked great. But making crazy choices can sometimes go very wrong.

~

The Polka Bus was a 1986 motor home with mauve interior and a rusted exterior. The inside looked like my bridal party and the outside looked like something that should have been in the movie *Vacation*. I had barely uttered the sentence to my father "I'm looking for better transportation for the band than renting a passenger van," when he called just twenty minutes later with the great news. "I bought one," he said.

"You bought one what?" I asked.

"I was driving down this country road after we hung up and I saw a sign "Motor Home For Sale", so I looked at it, and it was only $4,000, so I bought it. And the best part is, it only has 45,000 miles on it. It hasn't been driven in fifteen years!"

Now, anyone reading this who knows anything at all about motor homes is probably groaning at this point. The worst thing you can do with a motor home is not drive it. What I didn't know is even though it looked okay, everything inside was about to fall out or off. Every wall leaked and chunks of insulation would literally fall on us as we drove. The generator, which provided heat and air, worked one out of every ten times. And on every trip, something would break in the engine. I know nothing about engines. And none of my band members at the time did either. It was the textbook definition of "a piece of shit" and broke down on every trip. We started leaving hours earlier for gigs, allowing for roadside time. In the three years that I owned it, there was not one time when we traveled that something didn't break. Not one time.

Fed up with piece-meal repairs, I gave in, coughed up more than my dad paid for it, and put in a brand new engine. We headed out to play a gig in Albany, New York, when somewhere outside of Columbus, Ohio, around 5 a.m. I saw the temperature gauge go from C to H in a split second. I knew from experience that I HAD to turn off the engine immediately. I pulled off at the next exit, into what looked like an abandoned gas station. The tears were immediate. "This CAN NOT be happening to me again! I fixed it. I spent $5,000 so this wouldn't be happening! I fixed it. I fixed it!" I called my brother Lenny, who fixes cars in his spare time when he's not fixing lives.

Lenny and I had gotten extremely close over the years. He had become my personal counselor of sorts, keeping me grounded. He was the first one to whom I admitted I wanted to commit suicide. And instead of saying something like "No you don't, don't even think about it," he said, "You must be having a pretty shitty day." Validation can do so much more than stroke an ego. And when I called with the news that James had Down syndrome, all he said was, "I'm so sorry."

So it was natural for me to call him when I was stranded outside of Columbus, Ohio. Then he said what he always says when I call and I'm hysterical:

"I over E when it involves C. Intellect over emotion when it involves a crisis. You will make better decisions!"

"Okay, okay," I said, "What do I do?" "You're gonna have to get underneath there and find out if it is leaking oil, and if it is, you're gonna have to get it to a gas station, without driving it or you'll blow up the engine." Each one of the band guys woke up and came out to see if they could help, and knowing from past experiences that there was nothing they could do except wait for a tow truck, they went back to bed. I crawled under and confirmed it was oil. And as I lay on the hot cement, that's when I felt the first rumble. The kind of rumble you don't want to feel in your stomach when you're out in the middle of nowhere, sans restroom.

I crawled out, praying the feeling would pass, and saw a women wandering around the motor home. She was holding a roll of paper towels under her arm, asking if I needed any help. I was in such a state of frustration, sadness, cramping and hot sweats that her presence didn't register. I asked her if she knew where I could find a restroom. She pointed about fifty yards away, up a steep hill, to an independently-owned motel. Sidebar: Any road musician will tell you, the number one rule when traveling on a bus is that the bathroom is only for going number one. I was not about to be the one to break that rule, because I did not want the guys breaking that rule, since I was the one who had to empty the tanks.

I alternated between running to the motel so I could get there as fast as possible, to walking while trying to stop the...movement. "Fuck I over E," I screamed in the middle of the field. When I finally reached the motel there was a huge sign on the front door that read "BATHROOMS FOR PATRONS ONLY! " Are you kidding?

I begged the girl behind the counter for an exception to their rule. (If I would have had my wallet I would have bought a room!) She wasn't budging. I asked if there was a gas station nearby. In her very strong Columbus, Ohio, accent she said, "Oh, no, not really. It's pretty far." And then added, "Is that your motor home down there?"

"Yes," I said.

"Why don't you try the Asian massage parlor right next to where you are parked?"

What? Where? Oh dear God! It all made sense. The woman walking with a roll of paper towels under her arm, showed up after she saw the guys come out of the motor home. It wasn't me she wanted to give a hand to, it was the band guys!

I knocked on the back door of that "massage parlor" and asked to use the bathroom. As I was led through a maze of rooms and hallways, what I saw inside was heartbreaking. Teenaged girls lying on mattresses, barely clothed. I didn't know them, but I knew their faces. I recognized the emptiness, the sadness and the desperation. I locked the door behind me, covered the toilet seat with layers of toilet paper, sat down and I screamed at God, "Everything is broken. The Polka Bus. My Marriage. My son. And I can't fix anything!" When I quit screaming I sat in silence, watched a roach crawl across the floor, and I waited. I wanted so badly to hear something back from God. I wanted to know if I let go it would all work out. I wanted someone to tell me what to do. Instead, I got nothing.

I got behind the wheel. And with tears in my eyes and no GPS, I drove. To this day I can't tell you how I found or made it to that gas station. Despite my pissed-offness at God at that moment, He truly did take the wheel.

I filled the motor home up with oil, but because I was shaking so bad I spilled it all over the engine, which then caught on fire. I frantically got everyone out of the motor home, thinking it was going to blow at any minute, and torn because I was hoping it would. We doused the flames with the fire extinguisher I bought in case there was ever an emergency.

We made it to the gig in Albany and back home, stopping every couple of hours to refill with oil. I dropped the guys off in Nashville and turned around and drove the Polka Bus up to Cleveland.

I pulled up in front of The Nash. Most of the Slovenians had long since left the neighborhood and it had been sold a few years back to a church. I smiled as I realized that the building was still doing its job. Gathering people together and taking care of lost souls. It was still a safe place for people to be.

I drove by the house on Stanley Avenue. I couldn't believe how small and run down it looked. The flowers had been replaced by weeds. Layers of paint were chipping. And you could no longer see the white stone bench. It was as if the earth had swallowed it whole. It seemed years of neglect had taken its toll on everything from Stanley Avenue.

I pulled into my father's new house, handed him the keys and got the first Southwest flight home.

After a year of trying, my dad finally sold The Polka Bus for parts. It was dismantled piece by piece by piece. But what I learned in those three years of owning it, besides how to fix a break line with a scrunchie, is if you don't get to the root of the problem, no amount of patching will hold.

~

When Bob first asked me to do a timeline on my family history, the twelve months between July 1976 and 1977 were more than unbelievable. There were two babies (one of which no one knew was coming), two heart attacks, one lost dog and Lenny.

We celebrated the 4th of July in 1976 with fireworks that rivaled the display put on by the city. The backyard was full of friends and neighbors. My mom would stay in the house, listening to the police radio. And every so often she'd come back and tell us the cops were coming to shut us down. I'd throw down the cigarette my dad gave me to light my firecrackers and run.

Later that night, when the party was over, my mom lay alone in her bed. She heard the static and then the voices got louder. "Yeah we got a 10-50 with injuries. Motorcycle. South and Broadway. It's the Hrovat boy, Lenny. I think he's dead."

After getting high and drunk, Lenny ran his motorcycle into a telephone pole. He was thrown thirty feet from his bike and landed on his head.

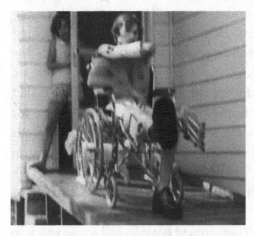

He came home in a wheelchair, with multiple physical wounds and a near-death experience that I would ask him to tell me over and over and over. He said he saw his whole life flash before his eyes in slow motion, then the most beautiful light he'd ever seen. He wanted to go to it, but he was hearing someone call his name. "Lenny, Lenny, stay with us." The policeman was shaking him, and then in an instant he was back in his body and filled with pain. We built a twenty-foot ramp off the back door and I loved to dance down it like it was a runway. But as Lenny's wounds were just beginning to heal, and his addiction to prescription pills was just taking root, there was more chaos.

It was almost a year to the date of Lenny's accident when my mom, dad and I went to a friend's cottage at Rock Creek, Ohio. I loved Rock Creek. And I loved our friends the Meljacs. Their daughter Denise was a year older than me, and we'd spend the afternoons skiing—in the water or snow—and spend the mornings visiting all the quaint antique shops in town.

One morning, my dad got up early and headed down to the lake to fish. Mr. Meljac went down about an hour later to join him. Not long after that, we heard sirens. When Mr. Meljac arrived at the lake, he found my father face down in the water, unconscious, and not breathing. For the next forty-five minutes he performed CPR, while shouting for help in between the breaths. Finally, someone across the lake heard his cries and called 911.

My mom and Mrs. Meljac headed down to the lake to see what was going on. When they got there, the EMTs were just putting my dad into the back of the ambulance. The man looked at my mother and said, "He's pretty much dead. We can't find a pulse." They continued CPR in the ambulance and somewhere between the lake and Ashtabula General Hospital my father's heart started beating again. As my mom followed the ambulance through the small town and winding streets, she witnessed the head-on crash. The ambulance carrying my father hit another car. The EMT said to my mother, "Look, I don't know how long it's going to take for another ambulance to get here, so we may need to put him in your back seat." But thankfully, a backup ambulance arrived from an even smaller town. However, as they drove, a thick billow of black smoke came from out from that ambulance, completely engulfing my mother's car. When they finally arrived at the small regional hospital, the ambulance died. They would have to call a tow truck to remove it from the emergency entrance.

Larry and Karie flew in. A party sprung up in our house in an instant. Family members and neighbors came and brought food and drinks. But my dad wasn't there to play. They begged me to get out my accordion. We danced the polka in the driveway. And it felt good.

For the next two weeks my dad would be seen by an array of doctors, specialists and psychologists. All of them said the same thing. First, it is a miracle he even survived, and second, if he lives, he will never be "right". He was in a withdrawal-induced coma. The shock on his system of not having any alcohol after thirty-five years was just too much. They also said we shouldn't hope for much; he would most likely be a vegetable.

Every day my siblings would go to the hospital to be greeted, not by my father, but a stranger. He was acting erratically, talking in crazy voices, and even foaming at the mouth. A real-life Linda Blair moment. Larry was deep in the charismatic movement of the seventies, and believed the devil was a living entity, which had now taken over my father's body. In his eyes, the only thing to do was to cast out the demon in Jesus' name.

Which they did.

Larry gathered some born again friends, and a few on-the-fence family members. And they laid their hands on my father and prayed. I wasn't there to see it.

The morning after the casting out ceremony, my siblings returned to the hospital to find my father, sitting up in bed for the first time in two weeks, drinking coffee, cracking his off-color jokes and flirting with the nurses. His normal behavior.

Larry will tell you God performed a miracle. The doctors were puzzled and offered no medical explanation. My dad doesn't remember any of it, so he would probably just tell you the one about the blonde and the computer. I'm going to play it safe and say all of the above.

We celebrated my father's fiftieth birthday in the hospital. He finally came home six weeks later and took his first stab at sobriety. The doctors told us as long as he stayed sober he could stay alive. But they didn't say anything about how to live with a sober alcoholic.

I was twelve. My mom would grab my arm as I walked past her in the kitchen and say, "Hey Kid, do me a favor, just go into the bedroom and make sure he's breathing." We were still all taking care of the alcoholic.

My dad became addicted to anything he could. At first it was TaB and Doritos. Then beef jerky. Then remodeling the house. And slowly, his occasional glass of wine at celebrations turned into every Friday night. Then wine turned into scotch and every day became Friday.

"It is only in adventure that some people succeed in knowing themselves – in finding themselves."
~ Andre Gide ~

11.

FIRST TIMES

I would lie on the couch and listen for the back door to open. My mom and dad would be coming home from a wedding at The Nash and I would run straight for my mom's purse. Because inside there would be napkin cake. A piece of wedding cake wrapped in a napkin. The cake was always sweet, but the best part was the feeling that she cared; that she thought of me enough to bring home napkin cake. It was like her love in a napkin.

Besides the occasional piece of napkin cake, dessert was not a big deal in our house. We were always more concerned about having twice as much klobasi than we needed. The priority was the meat. Well, that's not completely true. The priority was always the booze—then the meat.

But when I met Jim, I married into dessert. He comes from a family of bakers, so dessert was its own food group. Which is why, after twenty-plus years of marriage I now love dessert. I love dessert so much I have to ask to see the dessert tray before I order my meal, so I know how much room to save.

During the years I spent on the road trying to convince people to like polka, Jim became a successful television producer. He worked on shows for ABC and Lifetime, and with many country music acts. He created a show for Great American Country called *Short Cuts* and cast a then-unknown sixteen-year-old named Taylor to star in the series. The world would soon know her as Taylor Swift, and James would know her as the girl who bought him a life-sized teddy bear to welcome him into the world.

We were busy pursuing our dreams and we were fine. Which of course stands for Fucked up, Insecure, Neurotic and Emotionally unstable. And we were living parallel lives. I saw a Charles Schultz documentary one time where he said he felt like he and his wife lived parallel lives. They both went about doing what they loved to do and occasionally their worlds would cross. This rang true in my spirit. Jim and I obviously loved each other, but we only got as close as we needed to.

Broken relationships can work, especially if no one is trying to fix them.

Even in a dysfunctional relationship basic needs still get met, which satisfy us on a physical level. So it's easy to ignore the growing problems in order to keep getting those needs met. There is an odd comfort in the craziness, otherwise you wouldn't stay.

And then, before I knew it, we had been married for fifteen years. We celebrated our anniversary at dinner one night, and I could hardly think to order dessert over the very loud ticking sound. Jim's paternal clock. He wanted to be a dad. I had no ticking clock. But I felt like I owed it to Jim after all he put up with.

So, the next morning I went back and tried to find the God I met at nineteen in the chapel at ORU. I said, "Look God, I have no ticking clock, but Jim wants to be a dad. But I am so scared. Because I know what's coming. And I know I'm not going to be a good mother and I don't want to be a caretaker."

~

It was January of 2001 and I could hardly sleep that night. In the morning they would be announcing the 46th Annual Grammy Award nominations. I didn't think I could possibly get enough votes to get a nomination, but I hoped.

The announcements were made for the larger categories during a press conference that morning, and then Jim and I sat at our computers, hitting refresh, hoping to see the complete list, including "Best Polka Album". But back then computers were slow. After a half hour of trying, I went back to bed.

I wasn't feeling well and I thought I might be getting the flu. I had just laid my head on my pillow when the phone rang. It was KC. "Did you see?" she asked. "No, I couldn't pull up the list." Her tone changed. "Well, you got it! You got it! Congratulations! You are a Grammy Nominee!" There's no way to accurately describe those first few minutes. I literally fell out of bed as I crawled screaming to Jim, "We got it! We got it!"

The phone started ringing and didn't stop for the next two hours. Somebody made the comment that they thought this made me the first female in history to receive a Grammy nomination in the polka category. Jim started doing research to confirm this and it was true. This was no longer just about me, we were making history.

By noon the phone had died down and the adrenaline subsided a bit. I realized I still felt nauseated and I thought, "Oh shit, maybe I'm pregnant?"

I drove to Walgreens, bought a pregnancy kit and took the test, even though it said to use morning pee. I figured if I was, I was. I stared at the pink plus sign and my heart sank. I wanted to be happy, but I was so scared. This was the beginning of the end.

At three o'clock that day I had a production meeting. I had just taken a full-time freelance job as a producer on a show for CMT called *Inside Fame*. When I arrived, my dear friend Kent looked at me and said, "What are you doing here? You just got a Grammy nomination!" I reminded him that it was still polka and I would still need to make a living.

That night Jim and I went to dinner to celebrate the nomination. I put the stick in a box. I gave it to him and he said, "You're the one with the Grammy nomination, why are you giving me a present?" When he opened the box he was shocked but happy, and like me, slightly overwhelmed.

The Grammy nomination brought so many wonderful opportunities into my career in those next couple of weeks. *US Weekly Magazine* ran a story about me, I appeared on many radio shows and I performed for the first time on The Grand Ole Opry.

It was a magical moment. But as soon as I got off the Opry stage I ran to the bathroom. I had started spotting. It was Saturday night and I would have to wait until Monday to see Dr. Blake. I spent all day Sunday conflicted. I knew I was losing the baby. I knew I was supposed to be sad. But I was relieved.

The Grand Old Opry, 2001

On Monday morning Dr. Blake confirmed there was no heartbeat. And because of my age, she wanted to let my body naturally take care of the process instead of doing a D&C. We were in the midst of a public relations frenzy and there were numerous interviews to give and parties to attend. I carried the largest maxi pad they made in my small little clutch purse waiting for the inevitable to happen. I flew to Chicago for a photo shoot for the *US Weekly* magazine article.

I flew to Los Angeles for radio interviews. And I didn't leave home without my accordion and my maxi pads.

In the midst of the craziness we received a call from a producer at *The Tonight Show* whom I'll call Jane. Jane said they were interested in doing a roll-in piece with me. "Jay would take Lynn to the Beverly Center and we would have Lynn dressed in cool performance clothes and have shoppers try to guess which category she is nominated in."

My response to Jim was, "So they kind of want to make a joke out of polka?" He assured me it would just be a fun piece. I asked Jim to ask Jane if we agreed to do their piece, could we also get a music performance.

Jane laughed, "Listen, there's no way Lynn would ever get a music performance. She'd have to be Sting or Sheryl Crow. We only book musical guests who have major record deals." I told Jim to pass. He was shocked. He said, "Lynn, you do know you're turning down *The Tonight Show*?" I said yes. But I also knew I had worked too long and too hard to try to make polka music legitimate to now throw that all away for a few minutes on national television.

Jim reluctantly passed on the offer and Jane hung up the phone angry. And then she called back a week later. "Jay would still like to do this piece." Jim said, "Lynn would still like to play a song." It was still a no.

But then the stars got in line and everything changed.

I was standing in Water Tower Place in Chicago when my cell phone rang. It was Jim. "Lynn, are you sitting down? If not, I think you should sit down. I just got a call from Barbera, the talent booker on *The Tonight Show*. She said she can't make us an official offer until tomorrow, but she wants to know if she did make us an offer, could you be on a plane tomorrow to L.A. to play a song on the show on Thursday?"

My first thought was, "Take that, Jane!" followed by, "I am going to be the first person in history to miscarry live on national television."

I sat on a bench, trying to soak it all in, and I realized what a huge opportunity this was for me and my career. I made my way to the food court. I needed French fries.

A few hours later Dottie and I stood in a classroom at the Chicago School of Design. The girl we hired to design my first red carpet dress was just about to graduate. As we stared at the unfinished satin blue gown, we both saw the problems, and were a bit worried. But we also knew it was unfinished. The Grammys were still a week away and surely she would finish it by then.

I went into the bathroom to change out of the dress. I would love to speak highly at this moment about the cleanliness of the inside of that building, but let's just say that they must care more about cultivating the creativity of their students than they do about the janitorial services. The bathroom was disgusting. I carefully removed the pin-filled dress up and over my head, holding so it wouldn't touch the floor, and that's when I saw it. The blood was dripping down my legs.

Knowing I had been in the bathroom way too long, Dottie came in looking for me. "Are you okay?" she asked. My tears were all she needed to hear. I opened the door to the stall, and there, on that dirty bathroom floor, Dottie sat with me and held my hand. I don't know how long we sat there — five, ten, fifteen minutes, maybe more — but she held my hand and didn't let go until I was ready to let go of that baby.

I arrived home from Chicago. The next day, we put together a band. We rehearsed in the afternoon. I met a stylist at a trendy shop in town to buy clothes. Lots of clothes. Clothes for the performance, clothes for the rehearsal, clothes for the flight. And by 5:05 p.m. we were on the Southwest Air non-stop flight to Los Angeles.

I didn't sleep much that night. I got up and showered and dressed and then the phone rang. "Ms. Rink, this is your driver waiting to take you to the studio. Are you ready?"

I stared in the bathroom mirror. I was scared to death. Mostly because I believed I couldn't sing. And now I was about to do it on *The Tonight Show*. Some people can't stand the way their nose looks, or the shape of their legs; for me, it's my voice. I always thought I could sing well, until I was about eighteen and I sat in with a polka band in Cleveland. The bandleader looked over at me and said, "Don't sing, just play." That was it. Maybe he didn't want me to sing because *he* wanted to sing. Maybe he didn't want me to sing because he was jealous. I have no idea. But that day he planted a seed of insecurity that dug its heels in deep. I would spend the rest of my life trying to ignore, justify, forget and heal his one little comment. And if his comment was enough to derail my thoughts about my voice, how much more powerful were the millions of comments both spoken and unspoken that swirled around in my house as a little girl?

I looked at myself in the mirror. I tried to tell myself I could sing. I told myself that Barbera wouldn't have booked me if I couldn't sing. But I couldn't stop the tears. I was still cramping and bleeding and my hormones were running rampant.

Barbera recommended that we play one of my original tunes, "Come Back My Baby". I had written the song while working on the Marc Anthony HBO television special from Madison Square Garden. His infectious style was inspiring that day.

We rehearsed the song at least thirteen times throughout the day. I spent an hour in my dressing room trying to rest. Jim called his parents and asked them to stop at the liquor store and buy me some vodka. I remember thinking how ironic it was that they were the ones buying me vodka. The drink definitely calmed my nerves a bit. Along with the dozen chocolate chip cookies I ate from the deli tray.

As I stood behind the curtain listening to Jay Leno's introduction, I turned to the band guys and said, "How did we get here?"

I was told I was also going to get couch time. A few minutes to sit on the couch across from Jay and have a conversation. This was a huge opportunity to share more about polka music. But as the minutes ticked away, I knew that might not happen. Turns out that Jane was still slightly upset that we were able to perform, and she was the timekeeper on the segment right before my performance;

men playing body parts. The bit was dying a slow death, and yet she wouldn't end it, taking precious television minutes from my couch time. I'm pretty certain this was her ego at play. And I was sad to lose the couch. But I was still glad I didn't take to the first offer.

After the show, the producers took us to dinner. As I climbed into the limo and we pulled away from the NBC lot, I couldn't wait to call my dad. I remembered one of my first performances standing on his duckpin bowling machine in Lud's Tavern.

I was eleven and had only been playing a few months when I learned my mother's favorite song, "Glas Harmonike", a beautiful Slovenian waltz. Around midnight, sound asleep, I felt my sister's arms waking me. "Get up, get up, Dad wants you to come to the bar and play," Karie said.

"Now?" I asked, wiping the sleep from my eyes. "Okay!" I said, excitedly, and got dressed.

When I walked into the packed bar my dad looked at my mother, "Fix her hair," he said. With that, she licked her hand and ran it down the back of my head. A few seconds later he stood me up on the duckpin bowling alley. From the floor he yelled, "Play your mother's favorite song!" I told him I wasn't ready and that I had just learned it. "Augh, bullshit, play it." he said. After three starts and restarts, the bar got quiet. I tried desperately to hold back the tears. I jumped down off the bowling alley and ran to the car.

Lud's Tavern, 1976

On the drive home I begged Karie for some comfort. "Why wouldn't he let me just play one of the songs I knew well? Why did I have to play that song?" She said, "You know dad. You can never make him happy."

She was right back then. But as I dialed his number from the back of that limo, I hoped maybe this time I had. "Hey Dad, it's Lynn. I'm heading to dinner, but wanted to call and see what you thought of the show."

"What the hell did you do to your hair?" he slurred.

"What?" I thought maybe I misunderstood him.

"Yeah, what the hell did you do to your hair?" he slurred again.

"Oh. The hair and make-up artist for the show just straightened it."

"Is it going to be like that forever?" he asked.

"No dad, it's just a style. Did you like the show?" I begged.

"Yeah, yeah, it was fine" he said, "Maybe now something good might happen in your career?"

Jim saw the look on my face. He put his hand on my knee and said, "I'm sorry. You did great. He just doesn't get it, Lynn. You know he's proud of you. He just doesn't know how to tell you." I knew that. But knowing something doesn't automatically stop the pain.

The next morning my voice mailbox was full of messages congratulating me on a job well done and the ratings showed four million people watched the show that night. But it wasn't enough. All I wanted was one person to be proud of me.

I couldn't get out of bed. And I couldn't stop crying. The mean voices told me over and over how horrible my voice sounded and how worthless I was and how I was never going to amount to anything. And then, my friend Tracy called.

Tracy is kind and honest and honest, and that is not a typo. She is my astrologer friend who knows what the stars are up to and also knows her own voice better than most people I know. One time, after not seeing her for over five years, we met at Rosebud's in Venice Beach. We had just finished hugging when she took one look at me and said, "Wait, your birthday is in March, right? Oh my God I am so sorry - but you are totally fucked right now." Apparently the stars were all out of whack, which explained a lot. And Tracy is not afraid to call it like it is. I love this about her.

Tracy called the morning after *The Tonight Show* appearance to tell me how much she enjoyed my performance and I fell apart over the phone. When I told her about the baby and the miscarriage she said to me, "Hang on a second, are you telling me you have just had the lowest low of your life and the highest high of your life within forty-eight hours of each other?"

"Yes," I replied.

She said, "Dear Lord, no wonder you can't stop crying. Okay, listen to me. You're gonna give yourself a break. Do you have any idea what your hormones are doing right now? You tell those mean voices in your head to shut the fuck up. You are wonderful and you did great. Now, get your ass out of bed and go eat an In-N-Out Burger."

And I did.

Two days later, a slew of family and friends sat with me in Staples Center for the 46th Annual Grammy Awards. When they called another band's name as the winner of that year's Best Polka Album, I heard my dad, seated behind me, start to cry.

I turned around and said, "It's okay dad. Don't be upset. I'll try again next year."

He said, "Of course you will, because the only reason I'm staying alive is to see you win." And I would continue to chase that golden trophy with the hope that it would win me my father's love.

"There is one kind of shock worse than the totally unexpected.
The unexpected for which one has refused to prepare."
~ Mary Renault ~

12.

RUN

By the time James was born my dad could no longer play the accordion. It didn't matter much to James, because James actually hates the accordion. Absolutely hates it. When I play he will throw himself on the ground, cover his ears and begin to wail. When I would show up to play for his class at school, he would run out the door. At first, I couldn't understand why he would act this way. But then, after remembering how I recorded the entire *Party Dress* CD while I was pregnant, I think it may have had something to do with having an accordion on his head for nine months. How would you feel if you had an eighteen-pound accordion on *your* head for nine months? During my entire pregnancy, the two most prominent things he heard were the sound of the accordion and the sound of my cries. Surrounded by amniotic fluid, I'm sure the two were hard to tell apart.

I guess a part of me is slightly relieved that he doesn't like it. Because if he did, he would surely be like Benny, and the last thing I ever wanted was a Benny.

During the Polka Bus years, I used to play a certain gig in Pennsylvania and one of the fans would always be there with their son named Benny. Benny loved polka music and Benny had Down syndrome. The closer we got to the venue I could feel my anxiety grow, knowing I would have to interact with him. He would surely want to hug me and kiss me which was always an awkward moment. Then, Benny would stand next to the stage and dance for the entire show. I would try to ignore him throughout the night but he was hard to miss. One time someone in our group told him the way he held the tambourine would make the lights go on and off on the guitar pedal board. Benny stood there the whole night trying to do it just right. It was so cruel. I was cruel. I understood why kids on the playground are so mean, because they are ignorant and scared and trying to act bigger than their fear. It doesn't have to be Down syndrome or a Benny, but whatever your biggest fear is, that is where you stand the most exposed. Lenny says,

"When you are faced with a challenging circumstance you will either get real or you will run."

I ran that entire gig.

I told this story to Diane. I was slowly beginning to understand my inability to face so many things. Slowly. Emotional growth is hard to recognize. It's not like standing against the kitchen wall every year, drawing a line to mark your height. It's more like deciding to drive from L.A. to Nashville and being so consumed by the beauty and the scenery that before you know it, you're in Albuquerque. Not the final destination, but further along than you were before.

I felt so bad about my behavior towards Benny and my ignorance. She asked me, "Lynn, do you believe you have a soul?" I told her of course I did. Then she said, 'Then you must believe that James also has a soul?" "Yes," I said. "Then, what makes James' soul, or Benny's, any less beautiful than yours?"

When I got home I stared at James while he sat at the kitchen table eating his yogurt. It was easy to see his low-set ears and slanted eyes and large tongue. Was I really so shallow as to only see these physical things? Was I really someone who had lived her whole life on such a surface level? Was I really such a scared little girl to look at Benny with such disgust? The answer was yes. Yes I was.

I had lived my entire life from the outside in, not from the inside out.

I began studying as much as I could about the soul and tried to understand its essence. I bought and read every book with soul in the title. Like Thomas Moore's *Care of the Soul* and *Dark Nights of the Soul*. I fell in love with Wayne Dyer and during an episode of Oprah Winfrey's *Super Soul Sunday*, I heard him say, "The soul is the birthless, deathless, changeless part of us. The part of us that looks out from behind our eyes and has no form. The soul is infinite so there is no in or out of it. It is everywhere. There's no place that it is not." Which sounds beautiful and inviting. And then I heard him say, "When you judge another, you do not define them, you define yourself."

For the first time I saw the ugliness. I saw what years of shame and codependency can do to your insides.

People always ask me for the turning point in my healing, for the one big a-ha moment. For me, it didn't happen like that. It was a series of small a-has and awakenings. Diane calls them "windows of understanding", when you get a glimpse of something new, something different ... you will crack open the window of your soul and let new thoughts in.

~

The words came through the speakerphone and shot like an arrow straight to my heart. "It's a baby boy and he has Trisomy 21, Down syndrome," the doctor said. Silence. It was like the wind had been knocked out of me.

Like the time I fell off my white Schwinn bike in front of Auntie Jennie's house and landed flat on my back on the hot cement. I was sure I would never breathe again. Now, I hoped I would never breathe again. I gasped and then screamed from a place I didn't know existed. I felt internally sick, like my insides were being pulled out, one organ at a time, as if playing a losing game of Operation. Buuuzzzz.

I couldn't even look at Jim, but I heard him weeping from behind his desk. "Oh dear God. Why would you do this to us?" I thought. We awkwardly tried to hold each other, but there was no comfort in our arms. Sadness and grief circled around us, trapping us.

Moans and cries lasted for what seemed like hours. Then, the first words out of my mouth were, "Tell me what the Bible says about abortion!"

"Thou shall not kill," he said, without missing a beat.

"That's not good enough," I screamed. "That's not fucking good enough! I want to see that word – abortion. Show me where it says that I shouldn't abort this baby!"

I don't remember how I got to my bed, but I lie there for hours. I somehow picked up the phone and called Karie. We cried. I called Lenny. We cried.

Dying dreams flashed in front of my eyes like I was standing at Turn 1 on a NASCAR speedway. The moment I tried to grasp what I just saw, another one was on its heels. The baby boy, just eighteen weeks along, would most likely grow up and not drive a car, not get married. He wouldn't be a high school football star or win a Grammy.

Exhausted mentally and physically, I fell asleep. When I woke up, I reluctantly opened my laptop and did a Wikipedia search.

Down syndrome.

"Down syndrome, Trisomy 21, is a chromosomal condition caused by the presence of all or part of an extra 21st chromosome. It is named after John Langdon Down, the British physician who described the syndrome in 1866. Down syndrome is associated with some impairment of cognitive ability and physical growth. Possible heart defects. Low muscle tone. Poor eyesight. Delayed and poor speech. Severe to profound mental disability."

Page after page and photo after photo and thought after thought took me into a darker place. "I can't do this. I can't fucking do this! I don't want this baby!"

I never thought I'd ever consider abortion. Hiding behind an understanding smile I would internally be disappointed with friends who had them. But now, I got it. When you believe you can't do something, you should at least have the choice. You should have the choice to do what is best for you. I also knew these thoughts weren't coming from a spiritual place. It wasn't about being pro-life or pro-choice or Catholic or a born again Christian. It was just me, a girl, not wanting to have and care forever for a boy with an intellectual disability.

All I could see in my head were visions of Benny and others like him. People I believed were less than me and people who got made fun of and laughed at on the playground. And all I could hear in my head was that voice. The voice. You know that voice. It was a low-toned, slurred, non-understandable voice. The same voice that comedians use to mock people with a mental disability. That voice was going to be my son's voice! The pain was the worst I'd ever know. And then I typed...

...how to commit suicide.

I had been in bed for almost forty-eight hours straight when Jim came and sat next to me. I could tell by the look on his face he knew

I was searching for ways to die. "Look Lynn, I have a hard time believing someone else can raise this baby better than we can, but I don't want to lose you over it. Also, I did some research and there are organizations that adopt kids like this."

His words were like oxygen. Like he was giving me CPR. They gave me a way out of the darkness. They gave me an out. And they enabled me to at least get out of bed. When you feel like you are stuck and you are out of options, it's difficult to move. It's as if you are emotionally frozen. But when you give yourself—or your husband gives you—an alternative, even a bad alternative, you can start to wiggle. And things get looser. Like wearing elastic pants on Thanksgiving Day. You begin to breathe a bit easier, which lets in new thoughts.

Weeks, then months, went by. I never brought up the adoption option again. I'm not really sure why, except that my ego was too big to be *that* woman. The woman who gave away her not-so-perfect child. I could never survive people thinking so badly of me. Plus, after having baby showers that rivaled any Grammy party we ever had, there were way too many baby gifts to take back. I started ignoring that I was even pregnant. And I got busier than I'd ever been.

We started working hard on the *Party Dress* CD. We wrote a song called "Polka Till The Cows Come Home" and flew to Austin to record it with Ray Benson of Asleep at the Wheel. We hired the Grand Ole Opry singers to sing backup on the song "Happy Feet". We shot our first music video for the song "Squeeze Box".

A few years before this, a friend had suggested the idea of using the accordion as a dress for a photo. Now, while pregnant, it seemed like the perfect time to do

Courtesy Kisa Kavass

so. We hung the box from the ceiling and I stood behind it in a flesh-colored body suit, six months pregnant, trying to hide everything. I was stuffed into Spanx like a Slovenian sausage and I was sure my ankles and eyelids got fat. The photo session was a success and I was hopeful that this record was going to be the one that would win us the damn trophy.

One night I was driving home after another long day in the studio and I came to the stop sign about a half a mile from my house. And that's when I felt it. Kick. Kick. Kick. It wasn't the first time I felt the baby kick. The first kick was subtle, easy to ignore. But this time the kick was strong, as if trying to get my attention. "Shit that hurts!" I yelled. With my foot on the brake I adjusted my new one-size-larger elastic-waist jeans and tried to get comfortable. I hated being pregnant. People talk about a woman having that pregnancy glow but I just looked pasty.

I found out earlier that week I had gestational diabetes. Prior to this, the only thing making me the slightest bit happy was eating as much sugar as I wanted and now that would have to stop. I also had morning sickness — morning, noon and night. My back hurt. My boobs were huge and sore. But none of these physical ailments even compared to how badly my soul ached.

I saw the headlights approaching me from behind, adjusted my jeans again and then, the baby kicked once more. Harder. Stronger. With purpose. "Stop it!" I screamed, "I hate this! This is the worst thing that could have ever happened to me. You are going to be the death of me!"

Those words were barely off my lips when I felt their ugliness. They circled around me like a thick black fog, first shocking me then trapping me. I couldn't believe I said them. Teardrops landed on my belly and that's when I barely heard it. "You are so wrong, Lynn. This baby is not going to be the death of you; this baby is going to save you."

~

James sat quietly at the table eating his yogurt. I looked at him and thought about his soul. Who was he? Who was I? I had so many questions. James looked inside his yogurt cup. His spoon was too short to reach the few last bites. I watched him pick up the carton and try to get in through the bottom. He knew there was more yogurt in there and he knew he wanted it. He just didn't know how to get to it. So he tried another way. Of course, it didn't work, but I remember being so awoken to the clarity that we, as typical adults, don't even allow ourselves the freedom to try another way or different approach. We automatically assume it will not work. But James doesn't. His brain is open for any and all options. His faith is so big he automatically believes there's another way.

One of my favorite singers is James Taylor. And he has a song that talks about just that, which I listened to over and over and over. It tells the story of how the Magi, after visiting with Jesus at His birth, were warned in a dream of King Herod's scheme and had to find another way home. It may have been a longer path, but they took it and eventually got to where they were headed.

I was now officially in the "action" stage of change. And I was trying to find another way home. My own way home. I was beginning to realize that taking Lexapro was working; it was enabling me to look at life and James on a deeper level than I ever had, past the physical and into the spirit.

I am not a human who just happens to have a soul; I am first and foremost a soul, who happens to be living inside a human body.

"Life and death are one thread, the same line
viewed from different sides."
~ Lao Tzu ~

13.

LIFE AND DEATH

The big, round light above my head made me squint as Jim
bounced into the operating room, grinning from ear to ear. All I
could think was, "How the hell can you be happy at this moment?
I'm about to give birth to a broken baby."

I felt my stomach open, but it didn't hurt. Jim stood nearby. "Is
that her liver?" he asked. Dr. Blake pushed him back a bit. Then, I
felt a tug and she said, "Lynn, he looks good." What did that mean?
Did it mean that despite the Down syndrome he really didn't look
that bad? Or did it mean…?

I watched the nurse take him to the weighing table. She stood in
my line of sight. I couldn't see him but I heard his first cry.

Then I prayed.

You see, of all the tips I read and tried not to remember reading
in the *How To Raise A Baby With Down Syndrome* book, one was about

to be put to the test. It said that typical babies come into the world all curled up with their tiny fists tightly closed and their arms and legs drawn in close to their bodies, but babies with Down syndrome, because of their low muscle tone, their limbs flail in the wind like a lost kite.

I waited.

And then, as the nurse stepped away, I could almost feel the breeze travel through the operating room as his little arms fell off the table and lay wide open.

The nurse brought him to me and put him in my arms.

And I felt nothing.

Back in my room, we all celebrated. We drank wine and beer and ate pierogies and klobasi. Friends said things like, "Lynn, I promise, you can't even tell!" which I knew was a lie.

After everyone had gone, I cried for hours and hours and hours. I don't think I ever really slept that night. And I had never felt so lonely or so empty. I must have dozed off, because in the early morning hours I was awakened by the sound of the hospital phone ringing next to my head. "Hello?"

"See, God dammit – I told you he was gonna be okay!"

"Hey Dad," I answered.

"So, he's good, right? He's healthy, you're okay?"

"I guess."

"Eh, don't you worry about a thing LynnMarie, you just do what I told you, you're gonna be just fine."

I hung up the phone and I buried my head in the pillow and I screamed out at the top of my lungs.

"He's not okay, Dad! I'm not okay. Why can't you see that? Why can't you see me?"

James spent a week in the NICU due to low oxygen levels. It was very odd to have had a baby and to be released from the hospital but come home without one. That first week was a breeze. We were in the midst of some final tracks on the *Party Dress* CD, so I would go to the studio, then go to visit James, and then go back to the studio.

Before bringing James home, the hospital rule was that I had to spend one night alone with him in my room. I packed a bag and went back to the hospital. They set us up in a room on what appeared to be an empty floor. It was deathly quiet. The nurse got us settled, then left. I stared at James, sleeping in the bassinette and I had never felt more scared or more alone in my life. And I never hated myself more.

I was relieved when Jim came in the next morning. Relieved I hadn't done anything horrible. And relieved because I knew even if I were to not be here someday, Jim could handle taking care of our son.

For the next week pressure of the birth announcement weighed on me. It took us a whole day and hundreds of photos to find one that was the most least obvious. My dad was right; he was healthy, except for—that.

Karie came whenever she could to help with James. She was such a source of strength for me, even though her own life never got easy. Her first marriage ended because of alcohol. Her second marriage ended because of an affair. Her third marriage never happened because her fiancé died at forty-four of an abdominal aortic aneurysm. And then, at forty years old, she was diagnosed with breast cancer and fought to beat it. When my father's health began to fail in 2005, she and her new husband Tony made the decision to take care of my father full time. My dad moved into their basement and he lived there for the last four years of his life. I'd often wonder how she could do that. How could she care for him 24/7 after the broken heart he caused her? But codependency causes everyone to do things they surely would never do if they were thinking clearly. And maybe sometimes the wound is all you have.

Karie, Dad & Me, 1999

~

It was a Monday in July when Lenny called and said, "Lynn, if there's anything you want to say to him, or if you want to see him alive one last time, you might want to consider coming to Cleveland today. If you've said all you need to say, then don't feel that you have to come." I wrestled with his words for a couple of hours. Had I said all I needed too? Hadn't I spent a lifetime trying to say and get what I wanted? What would another hour provide that a lifetime couldn't? But what if this time he got it? Or what if this time I really forgave him? I made the decision to go, not so much for my dad, but for me.

He had come this close to death so many times before. One time, we all flew to Naples, Florida, where he spent his winters, to say goodbye. He was unconscious as we stood by his bedside and told him how much we loved him. In the morning, I had to leave for a gig. It happened to be Easter morning. I was waiting at the airline gate when I got the call from Jim: "Lynn, are you sitting down, because you're not going to believe this, but he has risen again!"

But this time, that wasn't going to happen.

In a way I had already mourned his death years before. I had watched his slow, painful demise, when his body began shutting down, even though his mind was sharp. It started with little things. First he quit cutting the grass and chopping firewood. Then, he was no longer able to do his daily walking loop around the neighborhood. He started to have hospital stays that lasted a month. Usually heart related, always alcohol accelerated. And every single time the doctors would tell him the scotch wasn't helping. But then, an emergency room doctor who didn't know his history would say something like, "A glass of wine now and then might be good for you." Might—if he wasn't a lifelong alcoholic. Might—if he could stop at one. But my dad took that suggestion as an order, except changed it to scotch, and nightly.

I knew twenty years ago that he wasn't going to quit drinking. How could he? Why would he? This was his life, the only life he had known. Stopping and dealing with why he felt like he needed to hide behind the alcohol was too old and too deep of a wound for him to tackle. I would beg him. But nothing I ever said was enough for him to choose me or anyone over the booze.

I spent my entire adult life learning how to deal with his drinking. I learned how to let his harsh words and disapproval go in one ear and out the other. Most of the time. Sometimes they took a pit stop between my ears and made me crazy. But the length of crazy got shorter. It went from years, to months, to days, then minutes. I'd hang up the phone after a call with him and I would say out loud, "He loves me. He loves me. He loves me. He just doesn't know how to show me. He's never known how to show me. He is proud of me. He is just a deeply wounded man who doesn't have the skills to go any deeper than he just did. Amen."

An alcoholic can only give enough to fill their need, not someone else's.

I don't want to make it sound like it was all bad. Sprinkled in between the frustrating times were fun times. Happy times.

And what he did for me on that first trip to Europe in 1989 enabled me to find my passion. He rekindled my love for music and entertaining, a desire that had been stripped away by the subtle spiritual abuse of a religious system.

I'd fly to Cleveland often for shows or big polka events. We'd hang out at the bar and dance and laugh. Everyone still loved Lud. But soon, earlier in the evening than anyone else, he'd be slurring his words and stumbling. He'd be yelling at me that the band was too loud and my vocal mic wasn't loud enough. He'd be frustrated that the bartender poured a weak drink. He'd be angry that someone wouldn't cough up fifteen bucks to buy one of my CDs. And that's when I began to mourn. I longed for the father who could have fun but not get drunk. The dad who could play his accordion without stopping between songs to drink. For the dad who could just be proud of me because I was me, not because I was playing the accordion.

The Beachland Ballroom, 2006

I knew the end was near when he lost his desire to play his accordion. I was playing a gig at the Beachland Ballroom in Cleveland. It's a great venue that was once a polka joint and now is a rock club that occasionally hires alternative polka bands to play there. We brought a stool up on stage for my dad. This time it was me who helped take the accordion out and secure the straps in the back. He talked to the audience and told them how proud he was of me and my success. But then he barely made it through one song when he stopped and said, "I'm gonna let my little girl take over." It would be the last time we'd ever play together.

Near the end of his life his skin had turned black and blue because of his diabetes. He was missing one big toe. He had open-heart surgery and thirteen stents which left him with only sixteen percent of a working heart. And he was still trying to learn to love.

I got on a flight to Cleveland and arrived that afternoon. I stood next to him, solemnly for a bit. Not quite sure what to say or do. Except I knew I wanted to be present. I didn't want to do what I did when my mother was dying, which was nothing. I wanted to be as close as I could. I swabbed his mouth with the wet pink sponge. I remember feeling a bit relieved he was dying. I knew he was tired of the fight. I curled up next to him in his bed and sang songs to him in Slovenian. I told him I was sorry I had never won the Grammy. I put the phone to his ear so he could hear James squawk one more time. I watched a single tear fall from his eye and I imagined it said all he never could.

The hospital phone rang. It was Larry. He couldn't make it home. He said his goodbye over the phone.

There's an awkwardness that happens when you are standing around waiting for someone to cross over. The spiritual part of you wants to be a firm believer the next place is better than the hell you've been living in. You want to believe in the streets of gold and the pearly gates and St.

Peter welcoming you with a shot of Slivovica. And yet, for me at least, this felt like the most faith-less time.

The priest came and gave my father his last rites and after he left it turned into a party, just like my dad would have wanted. People came and went, told stories, even drank cocktails. By 10 p.m., we were exhausted. Realistically he could hang on like this for days. So I got comfy in the hospital chair with a large white blanket over my legs. I opened up my laptop and put together a play list of some music I thought he'd like to hear.

I pushed play on my song "Forevermore", one of his favorites, when I heard my sister-in-law Gail, Lenny's wife, say, "He's gone."

I had missed it. In the only minutes when I wasn't watching, he had passed. I stayed in the chair but I looked up. I had seen once on a television show where the spirit floats above the room for a while watching everyone down below, before it leaves. I smiled and waved goodbye.

I didn't feel much of anything spiritual in those first few moments. I wanted to believe that he was going to heaven, but there was so much chatter in my head from past born again Christians saying, "If he wasn't really born again, then he is not in heaven." And then the Catholic thoughts of, "If he hadn't had communion in years, he's probably in purgatory and I need to cough up some cash to get him out." I sat on a bench outside his room while we waited for the coroner. And I decided to just trust how I felt. I told the mean voices to shut up. And I didn't try to think my way out. In that moment I felt that my dad was in a better place. I didn't know where it was or what it looked like, but I knew it was good. I had learned enough from James to know that we are first and foremost spiritual beings who happen to be living in human bodies. My father's human body was gone. But his spirit would most definitely live on.

But if I did believe there was an actual heaven and if I did believe that we are reunited there with our loved ones, then I felt happy he would finally be back arm-in-arm with my mother. They belonged together and he was never quite right without her. He had lots of lovely girlfriends through the years, but there was something about the bond he shared with my mother from the beginning that kept them connected, even in her death. Forever his protector, she would be there waiting for him with open arms. I remember watching them waltz across the room, any room, whether they were dancing or not. They belonged together. Filled in each other's gaps. And now they would be waltzing in heaven.

I know my mother deeply loved my father, and vice versa. Even in the midst of alcoholism and codependency and dysfunction. This

is how I feel about me and Jim most days. We are walking around with fifty tons of baggage on and around us, but we still love. Maybe that's the greatest form of love there is. The kind where you trip over shit constantly, but keep moving.

The next two days were a flurry of activity. Larry flew in for the funeral and the six of us siblings worked together on the arrangements. It felt nice and weird at the same time. Like someone brought down boxes from the attic. The memories were sweet, but they were covered in layers of dust and that dust gets all over you and up your nose.

Lenny had been named executor of the estate, so we all agreed "Head of Funeral Arrangements" fell under that category. He would decide on the wording for the memory card and choose the pallbearers. He said, "Dad pretty much carried each of us six kids at different times in our lives, bailing us out financially, getting us out of jail (or leaving us there), or paying for crazy career ideas, so I think it's only appropriate that the six of us carry him to his final resting place."

I thought it was an awesome idea. Like for some reason this was the only reason there were six of us! But because Lenny is also the man who says, "I over E" he added, "It's supposed to rain on Thursday. How will the girls carry the coffin in high heels and in the rain?"

Black plastic rain boots.

As the coffin was wheeled out from the funeral home the six of us walked alongside it, the boys intermixed between the girls in order to distribute the weight, and my sisters and I were wearing black plastic rain boots. And in true Hrovat fashion, we added an exclamation point to the already great sentence. Karie took white shoe polish that she found amongst my father's things and painted "WE *HEART* LUD" on the outside of each boot.

As we walked up the soggy hill that July morning to place my father next to my mother, there was no doubt about the amount of love we had for our dad. For a father who, even though he couldn't tame his own demons, through them and because of them, taught us to understand ours. KC got out her accordion and right there at the gravesite we sang "Tam U Dolu" and "Mi Se Imamo Radi", and danced.

It wouldn't be until a few months after he was gone that I learned the whole truth. Karie told me that when I first called my dad and told him the news that James would have Down syndrome, he cried for weeks. And he couldn't talk about me or ask about me without getting upset. And that for the very first time in his life, a smile couldn't hide his pain and a drink couldn't soothe him.

> *"The difference between friends and pets is that friends we
> allow into our company, pets we allow into our solitude."*
> ~ Robert Brault ~

14.

DOGS

Jim and I spent the first two years of our marriage living in Tulsa. Jim was finishing up his degree and I worked several odd jobs to make ends meet. We were broke, so for free entertainment we would go to the pet store at the mall and play with the puppies. I loved the cocker spaniels with their floppy ears and large paws. We would play with them for hours, until the staff would kick us out to close the store. I always felt this intense sadness when we left. On the surface, I was sad we were leaving them behind, but I was also sad in a deeper place. The place where old wounds live and breathe on their own without us even knowing it.

When Jim graduated, we both got jobs working in television for a ministry in San Diego. The same ministry where my brother Larry was working at the time. We loved living in San Diego. We spent every weekend on the beaches of Del Mar. Jim spent hours boogie boarding and I kept up my sunbathing muscles.

But as the years went by, we both felt the pull to be closer to our aging parents. We made the very hard decision to move to Nashville in the mid-1990s, to be closer to our families.

Jim's parents lived in Pittsburgh and we'd visit often. They had a five-year-old beautiful blonde cocker spaniel named Taffy. Taffy was spending way too much time in a cold, damp mud room, so she wouldn't get underneath the feet of Jim's aging grandmother who lived with his parents. We jumped at the chance to take Taffy off their hands and she became our child. Not "like a child" but our child. We didn't have kids yet, so I became one of those over-the-top dog lovers who had birthday parties for her pets, with hats and candles and dessert.

We had Taffy for almost ten years before we had to put her down. One of the hardest days ever. Her ashes still sit on a shelf nearby as I write this. Having pets is the most tangible opportunity we have to learn to love and to let go. In that room, as you are holding them close and they are taking their last breath, you swear you will never put yourself through this again. But then, the need to love and be loved comes back and you take the risk.

It was almost two years after Taffy's death when I finally felt ready. It was September when I started asking Jim for another cocker. I would spend hours perusing the Internet, searching all over the country for the most perfect one. I wanted one just like Taffy: calm, sweet, easy going—traits difficult to tell from a photo.

But then December came along with the results of the amniocentesis and the dog conversations ended. Everyone told me, "You don't want a puppy and a baby at the same time, especially when it's a special needs baby!" But I did. I did want a dog and a child and all the chaos. I wanted James to have a buddy like I did as a little girl. But I could tell that Jim wasn't up for that challenge.

Then we got the news and the dark cloud of Down syndrome was now permanently positioned over my head. I hadn't been up

and out of bed in two days, and the tears never dried up. Jim on the other hand cried for exactly twenty-four hours. Then he got up, got dressed, took a shower and went to buy a puppy.

Jim believes desperate times call for desperate measures, and says when he woke up that morning, he took one look at me and he knew he had to do something, anything, to get me to stop crying. Maybe his strength came from having a brother who had special needs. Maybe he knew that having a blue handicapped parking permit in the car was not the end of the world. Maybe he was just stronger than me.

That evening, around six, I dragged myself out of the bedroom to our bonus room. The room was in transition, changing from being Jim's office to the new brown and tan, bear-filled nursery. Amongst the half-built crib and file boxes, I sat at our computer. I researched more about Down syndrome and tried to find even one photo on the Internet where I didn't think the child looked goofy. I reluctantly sent an email, reaching out to our local Down syndrome organization, hating that I was now a part of this club.

I heard Jim walk into the room and from behind me he said, "Merry Christmas!" I turned around to see him holding a tiny black and white cocker spaniel with a red bow tied around his neck. "Merry Christmas, Lynn. This dog is going to be our constant reminder that life goes on," Jim said, as he placed the puppy in the palm of my hand. "Hey there, Fido," I said, letting my first smile in days slip out.

We had decided months before that our next dog would be named Fido, in honor of Jim's grandmother who had recently passed away. She called every dog, Taffy included, "Fido" no matter what the dog's real name was.

But as I held Fido, my feelings of joy quickly turned to concern. There was just something about him. He was trembling and scared, which was expected, but I could see trouble in his eyes. "I think he's gonna be a feisty one," I said.

"We have twenty-four hours to return him if you don't like him," Jim said. Fido seemed to know the gist of the conversation, as he looked up and with his tiny tongue licked my cheek. Could I really give him away? I was still trying to fill the void left behind by so many pets, and I knew that taking him back would leave yet another hole. I couldn't even bear the thought of it. And in a way, keeping a not-so-perfect dog would help me feel like I was paying my penance for old sins.

~

It was a hot summer day in 1970. I opened the back screen door and yelled inside, "I'm going up the street to the Bergman's house to play." And as I turned to let the door close behind me, Pierre, my gray and black poodle, got past me. I watched him sprint down the driveway and into the street and under the tire of 1968 green Chevrolet. I stood frozen. I wanted to run to him, but I couldn't move.

The next thing I remember is lying in my bed. And then, my father appeared by my side. It was the first time I recall my dad coming to comfort me. He begged me to stop crying. I couldn't. I wouldn't. Even at the age of five I understood that if I kept crying, he would stay. The more I cried, the closer he got. And that's all I really wanted. Finally, in his desperation to get me to stop, he said, "I will buy you a new Pierre, tomorrow!" And he left the room.

This story always came up in therapy. First with Bob and then with the others. And we would talk about how traumatic it must have been as a five-year-old to go through such an event. We would work through recognizing my need for my father's love and acceptance, and how his answer to my grief, maybe his grief too, was to just buy a new puppy. I understood all the important parts of this story. At least the parts I remembered.

But then one day, while retelling the story to Diane, she asked me, "What happened between standing in the driveway and lying in your bed?" All the years of therapy, all the times I thought I had healed this, and I never recognized the holes. Diane encouraged me to dig deeper.

When we are ready, we can turn tragic memories into stepping stones of growth.

After standing frozen for a bit, I watched Lenny scoop Pierre up off the street and head towards me with his limp body. I ran into the kitchen screaming and crying. I can't remember exactly who said it, but instead of being comforted or hugged, what I heard was, "Why the hell did you let him out?! What the hell is wrong with you? God dammit, how could you do this?!"

The incident wasn't bad and awful and horrible—I was.

It turns out my first childhood memory wasn't at all about the death of a puppy or getting my father's attention. It was about believing that I was, at my core, a bad person. A new dog arrived the very next day. He looked exactly like Pierre, but he acted nothing  like him. My brothers named him JB, after the whiskey that sat on the second shelf of my father's bar. He followed me everywhere and protected me. When Lenny would try to hold me down and tickle

147

me, now JB would nip at his heels. But JB had a bad habit of running away.

He was about four-years-old when he went missing one day. I was home alone so I had no choice but to call my father at the bar. My dad was angry, but agreed to go out and look for the dog. I waited anxiously, staring out the kitchen window, praying that my dad would find JB. About an hour later my dad pulled into the driveway, JB bouncing around in the back seat. I could hardly contain my excitement. JB was home!

My dad opened up the back screen door and JB ran into the house. When my father reached the foyer, I watched him pick up a six-pack of empty beer bottles that was sitting on the floor, and throw the bottles as hard as he could at the dog, knocking JB's paws out from under him. JB flew across the linoleum floor, yelped and limped away. I stood there, motionless, feeling like I was the one who had just been hit. I cried silently inside, not wanting my father to see my fear.

Those few seconds were just more bricks being laid in the foundation of my codependency. My needs, thoughts and emotions did not matter at that moment; all that mattered was not upsetting my father any further.

A few weeks later, JB ran away again, and I found myself with my dad on a hot July day in the front seat of our paneling-covered station wagon, driving up and down the streets of Maple Heights looking for my best friend. I secretly prayed the whole time that we wouldn't find JB.

And we didn't.

~

The first few weeks after my dad died were especially hard. I spent a lot of time napping on the couch, ignoring James and avoiding Jim, which was difficult to do because I hardly ever left the house.

One afternoon, I was trying to take a nap when I heard a cry come out of James' room. But then it stopped. This happened several times, but I was too lazy to get up and check on him. Soon, his cries got louder and louder. When I finally got up, I found him almost at the bottom of the staircase, his jeans around his ankles, a diaper full of shit and a dark poop stripe down the middle of every single step. I was angry with myself for not checking on him. I was angry with myself for picking light-colored carpeting. I was just angry.

I spent the next few hours cleaning everything. The stairs, James' room, his clothes, but days later I could still smell it. Everywhere I went the smell of shit was there. I kept scrubbing and cleaning and washing everything in sight, and I could not for the life of me find the source. Until Fido jumped up on my lap. The poop was on Fido's ears. I obviously wasn't looking in the right places.

This is how I felt about my years of therapy. Jim and I had gone consistently to try to work out issues, but we could never get to the source. We were never looking in the right place. And we spent and wasted a ton of energy on making things look good and staying busy. One of my favorite authors is Richard Rohr. He is a Franciscan priest and an internationally-known inspirational speaker and I have often heard him say,

> "Ignoring our true selves can be like staying busy and just rearranging the deck chairs on The Titanic."

> *"Grief is in two parts. The first is loss. The second
> is the remaking of life."*
> *~ Anne Roiphe ~*

15.

MISSING PIECES

By the time fall came around I was feeling slightly better about being alive, which is to say I was only contemplating suicide about once a week. James was three-and-a-half, and just trying to walk, and I felt like I was beginning to stumble less. I decided to take James to Seattle for fall break.

I love Seattle and I love our friends, John and Karin, who live there. We met in college, soon after Jim and I were married. I have fond memories of scavenger hunts and one-dollar movies. Karin and I would spend every Saturday at the flea market together. John was a business student who worked at the television studio with Jim and me, and Karin was in the nursing program. After college she became a NICU nurse.

We remained close for many years after college until the birth of their first daughter. It's not uncommon for couples to grow apart when kids enter the mix, but that wasn't the problem. The problem was my inability to accept Gracie.

Karin and John's first daughter, Grace Heather Williamson, was born with a rare chromosome disorder. She is literally "one in a million", missing the 13th chromosome. Her needs surpass James' by light years, which always makes me thankful and embarrassed at the same time. Thankful for James' level of okay-ness and embarrassed about my behavior.

Karin knew early on in her pregnancy that something wasn't quite right. Her ultrasound revealed a rare genetic disorder, so severe the doctors were confident the baby wouldn't survive the pregnancy. Karin spent most of her pregnancy knitting a blanket in which to bury her unborn child. But at eight months along the baby was still living when Karin went into labor. The doctors then assured her that once the baby arrived, she would surely die within minutes of being born. But minutes turned into hours and hours turned into days. The doctors were dumbfounded. "We don't know what to tell you," they said. "We were sure she would die. This is a miracle." Gracie didn't die and Karin and John were bringing home a little girl, without ever having prepared to do so. But God put everyone to work and when they walked into their home, a nursery had appeared out of love.

It was truly a miracle story. One that I couldn't even get close to. I withdrew from Karin, from our friendship, at a time when she needed me most. I was so full of fear, and by this time convinced this was, in fact, going to happen to me, that I thought if I stayed far enough away, the reality would also be far away. But the opposite is true.

Karin and John went on to have three more typical children, Michael, Rosie and Anna, and because they had so much love to give, they adopted not one, but two beautiful girls from China, Summer and Emily. If you stand in their kitchen for five minutes you will be overwhelmed, tired and surrounded by love.

Their home in Stealicoom overlooks Puget Sound. It is part Pottery Barn and part barn. Warm. Rustic. Riding boots piled up at the back door for when it's time to feed the horses. They have dogs and cats and rabbits and chickens and goats. I have trouble taking care of one dog. But Karin seems to handle all of this with such grace. When I'm near her, I stand close, hoping her strength will rub off on me.

Number eight in the Twelve Steps program says, "Make a list of all persons we have harmed and become willing to make amends to them all." I knew that apologizing to Karin was on my list. I told her how sorry I was that my fear got in the way of our friendship. I told her how sorry I was that I wasn't there for her when Gracie was little and that I was a shitty friend. We hugged and I was never so thankful for someone's forgiveness.

Karin agreed to watch James for a few days while I journeyed a bit further north to Hoodsport, Washington, for a writing retreat. As I watched life and bodies and animals swirl around me I thought, "Well, none of her kids are dead or injured, how bad could it get?" I ate a few eggs that Karin just, I mean *just*, brought in from the chicken coop. After one bite I made myself a note to check our homeowners' association policy regarding chicken coops. I kissed James goodbye and told him I'd see him in a few days.

On the first morning I decided to go for a hike. I am not a hiker. I don't own hiking boots and I don't carry a water bottle. So I guess that makes me a person who walks in the woods. I found a trailhead off of Highway 119 near Hoodsport. It was a short, 1.5-mile loop at the edge of the Olympic National Forest. I had only been on the trail about a hundred yards when I came upon a makeshift shrine. There were a couple of candles and some flowers sitting on a stump. On the tree were stapled two pieces of paper, covered in plastic. The top was a photo of a beautiful white Akita dog with the name Meehah underneath it, and in big block letters, "MISSING". Below was a handwritten letter. The letter read, in part, "I don't know why things like this happen, but know that you added so much joy to our lives in the two years you were with us, and we learned more from you than you could ever imagine. Love, Mommy."

I sat next to the shrine and felt so bad for both Meehah and Mommy. I thought about that little dog, obviously lost in the woods. Whatever it was that initially drew him away, at some point he missed his mommy and wanted to come home, and just didn't know how to get there. I wondered how long he wandered. And I thought about his mommy, knowing the pain and anguish she went through while searching and then finally letting go. This is tough stuff, I thought. This is the stuff life is made of—and it's hard. Sometimes we get to choose our path and sometimes the path chooses us.

As I admired all the beauty around me, I noticed something I had never seen before. A tree had fallen on the path right in the middle of where people would need to walk. The park ranger had cut about two feet out of this fifty-foot fallen tree so people could get by. Instead of moving the entire tree, which would obviously be a huge task, they just took out a big chunk so I, and others, could keep going. It was obvious these two tree trunks belonged to each other, and even with the missing piece it still seemed whole. Sometimes the missing piece just allows us to keep going. It stays a part of who we are forever.

Losing something can be exactly what we need to happen in order to move on.

My sister Karie has become my constant reminder of letting go and moving forward. For thirty-three years she wondered about her child, born in secrecy and given up for adoption. Taken from her by a choice my father made. She never even got to hold or touch her baby. Her loss was great and the anguish was enough to keep a heart broken for life. I thought about my nephew and where he was and who he might have become.

As I walked, I started to feel extremely vulnerable. I was alone in the woods, and I hadn't told anyone where I was going. "What if I tripped and broke my ankle?" I thought. "No one would know where I am. I could be stuck in these woods for days. Or I could end up like Aron Ralston."

I love the Aron Ralston story. I first read the book and then saw the movie *127 Hours* at least three times. In 2003, Aron went on a hike in a remote desert canyon in Utah. A boulder weighing one thousand pounds fell on his arm. After being trapped for five days he knew his only chance of survival was to amputate his own arm to free himself. I can't even begin to imagine that kind of pain, both emotionally and physically. But he did it, because he knew that missing an arm was the only way to not lose his life.

I don't know why Mommy lost Meehah, but I am sure her loss will remain a part of her being forever. She will find a way to go on. And from the sound of her letter, she will soon be loving on another adorable creature. I can only believe her missing piece will make her an even better mommy. And I'm sure Aron still wishes he had his arm. I've heard amputees say they still physically feel they have their missing limb. But my guess is that Aron still feels whole, and in place of what he's lost, he has gained so much.

I made it through the 1.5-mile loop no problem. And I left Seattle with a new appreciation for my losses in life. I saw how Gracie added to Karin and John's life instead of taking away. I began to see my losses as necessary steps in my healing process instead of just bad things. From the animals I've said goodbye to, to all my unreached career goals, and of course the dream of a typical child. I had a renewed admiration for Karin's journey and for my sister's.

~

After my father died, Karie made the decision to search for her first-born son. It was time to get out from underneath the shame. She called one day with the good news: "Lynn, I found him!" Thomas Michael Zelski was alive and well and living in Chicago. Karie found her son, thanks to a kind soul at an Angel Network who went above and beyond the call of duty. She told Karie that there was someone on Facebook with the exact birthday as her son and maybe she should start there. Karie reached out to him via Facebook and got the response, "So, are you saying we are related?" Thank you, Mark Zuckerberg. Just a few days later, Thomas drove through the night from Chicago to Cleveland and showed up on my sister's doorstep. They wept in each other's arms, and Karie held her baby for the first time.

Within a few weeks, I headed to Cleveland to meet him. I stood on the jetway and I prayed for a safe flight. I was shocked. For years after James was born, every single time I boarded a plane for a gig I hoped it was my out. I secretly wished the plane would go down and it would all be over. But something had shifted. I felt different. The smallest part of me wanted to live. I heard this melody in my head and the lyrics came right along with it.

> *Welcome home hope, baby where've you been?*
> *It's so good to see you comin' round again,*
> *it's been a long and lonely road without you here.*
> *Welcome home hope, baby have a seat.*
> *And don't you ever think about leaving me.*
> *You're the only reason I still breathe.*

Meeting my nephew for the first time was like holding on to a living example that loss and pain can sometimes end in joy. That when you are in a bad place, the journey might just not be over yet.

We spent the entire weekend getting to know each other, and Karie got to retell her story. I asked for details because I was ready to hear them and she was ready to share them. She told me about waking my mom up at midnight, and the phone call to the bar and the ice storm. She talked about being alone when she delivered. When I asked what time my parents finally arrived at the hospital, she said, "Lynn, Mom never came to the hospital." My mother never got out of bed. My mother never got up. She stayed at home and she buried her head in her pillow. I was shocked and disappointed and disgusted. I felt anger towards my mom like never before. How could she do that to her child? How could she hide? How could she run?

And then the window cracked and I understood.

It's so much easier to forgive someone when you understand their pain.

I understood because I knew her. I knew how she felt. I knew how scared she was. I knew had she gotten up, it would have been the beginning of the unraveling of everything she was working so hard to keep together, and everything would fall apart. It was easier to bury her head in her pillow.

Karie named her son Michael, after grandpa. She thought that since grandpa had been a survivor, coming to this country alone, maybe Michael would be too. She never held him after he was born and within a day the baby was sent to Catholic Charities of Cleveland. A week later, Karie and my mom went to sign the official adoption papers. Karie stood by the door, within a few feet of her son. The nurse asked if she'd like to hold him. As Karie reached out her hands my mother said, "Don't you dare! Don't you dare touch him! If you touch him, you will want to keep him, and I am not raising another child."

Just kids themselves, Karie and her boyfriend broke up after the baby was born. She married a different man right out of high school, trying to escape the chaos and the memories, and quickly had two other children. When her children were old enough to understand, she told them about their half-brother. But apparently they weren't old enough, or seasoned enough, to understand how family secrets work.

One Christmas Eve, with the whole family gathered, the kids were talking. And in a child-like competition game, one of my nephews said, "My dad is so great, he shot a deer once." And my other nephew, Karie's son, Mark, says, "Oh yeah, well that's nothin'…my mom had a baby at seventeen!"

You've never seen full-grown adults scatter so quickly. We were like cockroaches when the lights were turned on. And no one said a word.

My father made a horrible choice because of his pain. That pain was passed on to my sister, and was a hurt she carried her whole life. But now it was out in the open in the light. And where there was once only loss, there is now a family. And more family. Thomas married his love, Katelyn, and my sister now has a grandchild. The story wasn't over, and now the story continues. His name is Tripp Michael Zelski.

Thomas, Tripp & Me

> *"Since we cannot change reality, let us change the*
> *eyes which see reality."*
> ~ Nikos Kazantzakis ~

16.

HOLIDAYS

I received an email and the subject line read, "The Baby Has Arrived". Dottie and Jamie were the proud parents of a baby boy. At first I wasn't sure about receiving such news via an email. There's something about hearing a voice on the other end of the line say, "It's a boy!" but on the other hand, I was so glad it wasn't delivered in person, where they might actually see all the horrible things I was feeling.

An instantaneous moment of joy was followed by jealousy. "Why do they get to have a typical child and I don't?" Then came anger. "God, it's not fair they get to have a little boy who could grow up to be president and I don't." Then grief. "At forty-five, are all my eggs are dried up and am I too old to even have a typical child?"

After sulking for a bit, I knew I had to get to the hospital as soon as I could.

I hadn't been in a hospital since my dad died, almost eight months prior. While the newness of his death was gone, the long-term missing had started.

When I finally reached the room, Jamie's parents greeted me. They drove up from Birmingham to be there as soon as they could. What makes this amazing in and of itself is that his parents have been divorced for over fifteen years. His father had remarried and his new wife came too. All three of them. Waking before dawn, driving in a car together for three hours, to see the baby.

As Dottie handed me this precious life, just twelve hours old, in the awkward yet careful transfer, our hands met underneath his small body. I remembered the feel of her hand, when she sat with me when I said goodbye to my first baby in that dingy Chicago bathroom. Now, I was getting to hold her first son.

As I held onto baby Beckham, I let go. I felt a softening in my heart. I realized I will probably never completely get over the death of my dream of a typical child, but I can, in the midst of that loss, still love. I let go just a little bit more of the anger and the fear. I saw in that newborn's eyes how new life can make you look at the future in a way you didn't think possible, and most importantly, new life can make you look at the past differently, so differently you will put aside years of hurt and get in the car with your ex-husband and his new wife.

The windows of understanding were happening more and more and I was slowly getting healthier. I knew I had turned a corner in my recovery one day when I made the decision to hang up the phone.

I was on the phone with a friend and it turned into an argument. And I knew in my gut that it was never going to be resolved. So, I hung up. I had bravely decided to take care of myself. The person on the other end was no doubt mad and angry and sad. But for the first time I listened to my gut and made the conscious decision to not act codependently.

In Melody Beattie's book, *The Language of Letting Go*, she writes the following, which was becoming my mantra:

"Boundaries emerge from deep within. They are connected to letting go of guilt and shame, and to changing our beliefs about what we deserve. As our thinking about this becomes clearer, so will our boundaries. Things change, not because we're controlling others, but because we've changed." [p. 3]

It was a baby step. But it felt huge and I was unprepared. It was like deciding to run a marathon without owning sneakers.

Acclaimed author Dr. Henry Cloud often says,

"We change our behavior when the pain of staying the same becomes greater than the pain of changing."

I understood my shame enough to stop being a slave to it. I set up boundaries with everyone in my life: family, friends, colleagues and Jim.

I had spent several years in therapy alone with Diane, and I was finally ready to commit to going back into counseling with Jim. We found a wonderful therapist named Don. One of the best things about Don was he understood the religious culture and belief system Jim was raised in. He also understood the spiritual abuse we lived under while attending ORU. He is a well-known Christian author and holds a Ph.D. in Marriage and Family Therapy. I always tell people it could take a few tries to find the right therapist. I never expected that, for Jim and me, it would take twenty years.

Jim and I learned so much about our marriage while working with Don. We learned we were two very young kids who both brought a ton of baggage into our relationship from the beginning. And we didn't have the skills to understand any of what we were carrying around. And the hurt we caused each other was not intentional. The hardness between us began to soften. The hurt began to dissipate. And this allowed the healing to begin.

We learned how to communicate our needs and desires. And we are still learning how to forgive, both each other and ourselves. We don't have it all figured out, but we've grown enough to be able to be a support to each other instead of being a hindrance. And most importantly, together we're learning how to care for and parent James. Which is challenging and exhilarating and always a learning experience.

~

The lady in the aisle at Party City held up the Superman costume and in an intense southern drawl said, "Isn't this the cutest thang? My little boy is going to love trick-or-treating in this! What is your child going to be?" She had no idea that standing next to her was a mom, a Northerner, an ego-centric artist, who was still full of anger, bitterness and fear, and that she was about to get punched in the face.

James hates Halloween. He does not eat candy. He is uncomfortable when he meets new people. And he doesn't like to dress up.

You would think that these issues would be enough to deter me from making him participate in the holiday. But every year, in my attempt to look and be as typical as possible, we wrestle James into a costume; we force him to walk up to people's houses with cobwebs and black cats on the porch, to collect candy, which only I will eat. Then, we find ourselves at the end of the night exhausted and crabby and full of commitment to never do it again. But like diets, addicts in withdrawal and childbirth, we forget the pain and dive in again. So, every year I walk the aisles at Party City, alongside other mothers as they hold up outfits of what their children will "be". A policeman. A fireman. A doctor.

But this year I hit the jackpot when I found an orange and black T-shirt that read, "This IS my costume". Success. I overcame the wardrobe issue, but I was not letting go of the rest of the festivities! "My child will still trick-or-treat!" Insanity is doing the same thing over and over and expecting different results.

As I pulled the shirt over James' head, the mean voices arrived. "You know, not only will James never want to dress up as Superman, or a doctor or policeman, the truth is that James will never be any of those things. He's going to just end up bagging someone's groceries or sorting bins at Goodwill. In fact, your son will never be an anything great."

I brushed the tears from my cheeks and I sat still in the silence. And God showed up in His perfect timing and delivered an a-ha moment. I was learning to listen more and more to my gut. "You know Lynn, James will not be a lot of things in his life, but the good news is that James will not be a lot of things in his life! He will never be a pessimist. He will never have prejudice. He will never be full of anger." It was a beautiful moment of clarity. But... did I mention I'm a slow learner? The rest of the evening went as it always did. Filled with James' resistance and me devouring of a ridiculous number of Reese's Peanut Butter Cups.

When the night ended and I lie next to James in bed, my stomach ached and my spirit was exhausted from the charade, and I wished so badly things were different. I thought, "James, I wish you were more like me." And it was as if I could immediately hear God's full-out belly laughter: "Are you fucking kidding me?" (Of course I don't believe God would swear, except when He's talking to me.) "Do you really want your son to be like you? Really? Do you want him to be oh, let's say, a cynic? A critic? Jaded? Full of fear? Angry? And a chocolate addict?"

I knew I didn't. I knew I didn't want James to be any one of those things, and I knew I didn't want to be any of those things either.

Halloween was barely over when the mall was decorated for Christmas. We decided to take James to see Santa the day before Thanksgiving, hoping to beat the holiday rush.

We got there before they opened and we were third in line. Soon, a family of five came up behind us and from the conversation I overheard on the adult level, I'm guessing the mom and dad didn't have the greatest of mornings, which was taking its toll on the kid level. Everyone was cranky and the father kept pulling out the old "Santa's watching you and he knows" line. I was glad James is clueless to this form of manipulation.

One of their little girls who looked to be about three, came around from behind her mother's leg and saw James sitting in his stroller. She stopped dead in her tracks and made a disgusted face, which included a lip curl, and said, "Ewwww."

I became the Grinch. I clenched my teeth. I thought of a million ways I would ruin this little girl's Christmas. I started to do the math in my head at how much it would cost me to get out of jail if in fact I did haul off and punch her in the face. Could I afford bail? And would I be out in time to eat Thanksgiving dinner and bow my head and try to be thankful for having a child with Down syndrome? I could see the newspaper headline: "Nashville Mother Of Boy With Down Syndrome Arrested For Assaulting A Three-Year-Old At Green Hills Mall". I didn't care. I was so pissed. I thought about saying something clever to her parents like "You all might want to fix your attitudes first and then fix your daughter's," or something kind, like, "I hope you choke on a turkey bone tomorrow," but I didn't say anything. I looked down at James, who was singing his garbled rendition of "The Itsy Bitsy Spider". I realized this was the first time I had turned into a protector. And I was surprised.

As I stood in line, trying hard to come to grips with all I was feeling, I knew this was a lot of my own shit. I knew the girl was only three and James may very well have been the first special needs child she had seen up close. I was mad that the five-year-old inside of me was still wounded by seeing a stick in my stocking. I knew I was angry because I am nowhere near strong enough to tell the parents what just happened or to confront the situation. Because, I knew that there was still a very real part of me that thinks, "Ewwww" as well.

When it was finally our turn, Jim and I geared up for the five minutes of craziness we were about to endure. We always have to have a strategic plan: "Okay, you take care of the camera and the stroller, and I'll take care of James."

I looked at Santa and I said, "You're basically gonna have to hold him at the waist with all your jolly might."

I set James on his lap; James did the arched back move, as Santa tried to hold him. I could tell he was shocked at how strong James was. "I told you, all your might." Then, I start the run and duck game. Run in, tickle James' stomach, run out and duck below the camera, with the hopes that the lady with her finger on the trigger is quick. Turns out, not quick enough. So we did it again, and again and again.

My face was pressed against the floor, partly from exhaustion and partly to stay out of the camera shot when I remembered Diane's words. "Lynn, is this really about James or is it about you? Is it about your need to appear typical? When are you going to stop looking at James' life through your eyes, and start looking at life through his eyes? He needs so little to be happy." With my face on the carpet, I began to cry. This had nothing to do with James. He doesn't know who Santa is, doesn't have a list of wants to read to him with the hopes that he'll deliver, and could care less about the damn photo. But I do. I want that great shot of James sitting on Santa's lap and smiling so that we can mail it to all our relatives to say "See, we are just like you!"

I stood up and looked like I had just run a marathon. I was sweating and disheveled when Santa walked up to us and said, "I just want to shake your hand. You guys are doing a really good job at a really hard job and you have a very special boy right there, and I believe God has a big purpose for his life!" Then I saw the tear in Santa's eye.

By the time spring came I felt even more hopeful. It was Easter. And Lenny and Gail and their kids would be in town for the holiday. I was happy to get to cook for them.

As I waited in the checkout line with my groceries at Publix, I realized the bagger was a boy who had Down syndrome. I immediately tried to go to another line as to not have to face him, but there were two people behind me and backing up a train is not easy. So I was forced to stay.

In front of me was a grandma with her obviously overtired, sugar-filled grandchild. And then, as if the world tilted just a bit too far on its axis, everything went terribly wrong. I watched the boy with Down syndrome enthusiastically smile at the little girl, at which she broke out in a bloodcurdling scream, followed by yelling, "Arghhhhhh make him stop, he's scaring me! His face is scaring me!" The grandma was mortified, and several Publix employees came by to see if they could help, but the little girl would not stop. My heart started racing and I felt like I might throw up. Not because of what the little girl was doing, but because I *was* that little girl. I took a deep breath and I remembered, "It's so much easier to forgive someone when you understand their pain."

> *"The feeling remains that God is on the journey, too."*
> *~ Saint Teresa of Avila ~*

17.

A NEW DRYER

I spent two full years in therapy with Diane. I thought I was doing pretty well. I was acutely aware of my codependent nature. I was taking only half a Lexapro a day. And I sat in my robe only in the mornings. I felt like I had done a good job recognizing my shame and healing it. I was even learning to forgive myself. It was the future that still scared the hell out of me.

I found myself back on Diane's floor, once again covered in snot. "I know James is a cute little boy now. But he is going to grow up and be ten, twenty and thirty and the world is going to be cruel to him. What kind of life is he going to have? And who is going to be with him to hold his hand when he's about to leave this world?" I wanted a concrete answer from her. I wanted absolutes. But instead she asked me a question. "Lynn, you talk a lot about life in the future. Have you ever thought about now? You told me that James wakes up happy and he goes to bed happy. Have you ever thought about just living life in this moment?"

The truth was, I hadn't. Even though I had spent the past two years in therapy. Even though I was making better choices. My daily thoughts were still consumed with what was going to happen in the future. Until the day my dryer broke.

I had thrown in my wet clothes and turned it on, and then a huge spark shot up from behind, followed by a plume of smoke. It was the last thing I needed at the end of a really bad week. Too many arguments with Jim (even though he was out of town), too many frustrating moments with James (because Jim was out of town), and too much pee on the floor from Fido.

I took my wet underwear out of the dryer and laid them on the patio furniture in the sun to dry, and I started yelling at God. "Why do bad things keep happening to me?" I screamed. I tried to explain to Him that I was doing all the right things: going to therapy, reading self-help books, trying to be a good mom. I felt like I had made so much progress in my journey of understanding who James was; who I was. But I still felt like He had a huge magnifying glass up in the sky aimed right at me, with the sun bouncing off of me at just the right angle, like an ant about to get fried. I poured myself a mojito, even though it was 11 a.m. on a Sunday.

I called my brother Lenny for advice on the dryer. He could tell by the sound of my voice that this wasn't just about a broken dryer. He reminded me of "I over E", and after hearing the symptoms and age of my dryer he said, "Go buy a new dryer."

Then I got excited. If I was going to need to buy a new dryer, I was going to get the Electrolux-Deluxe-Kelly-Ripa-everything-is-perfect-dryer! My life was going to be just like the commercials. I was going to have the perfect biceps, make the perfect cookies and throw them to the perfect-looking kids!

When James woke up from his nap, we headed to Sears. I remembered to put him in the car. A true sign there was progress.

Sears happened to be having a promotional sale that day, so they had popcorn, balloons and a band set up in the parking lot. "Oh,

I've played a lot of crappy polka gigs in my life," I thought, "but I never had to play a Sears parking lot in 95-degree heat! We will come support them when we're through."

Pushing James in his stroller, I headed to the appliance section and I found the saleslady. Somewhere between home and Sears I had decided that if my dryer was broken, the washer was probably soon to go, so I might as well just buy both. I told her with sheer excitement that I wanted to buy the Electrolux Deluxe. I'm sure it was obvious this was about more than just a dryer. I stood staring at the most beautiful piece of stainless steel I'd ever seen; it came with all the bells and whistles and even angels singing. "Would you like me to write it up?" she asked. Back in my body, I asked for the price. Everything in me wanted this perfect dryer, and the perfect life, but I knew financially this was not the best time to purchase. "I think I'm gonna need the I-don't-do-anything-but-dry-clothes-dryer," I said. "Oh," she said, obviously disappointed, "those are over here."

As I stood in front of the stark white Maytag dryer with only two buttons, an elderly woman approached me. I had seen her, kind of stalking me, the whole time I was in the store, and now, with tears in her eyes she walked up to me and asked, "Is this your son?" I nodded.

She proceeded to tell me that she had just lost her little boy. "He was sixty-one years old when he died," she said. "And he had Down syndrome. They told me to put him away, but I didn't, and I took care of him his whole life." Then she leaned in a bit closer and asked, "Can I tell you something?"

"Yes," I said, feeling the dam of emotions inside me about to break.

"I know how hard it is right now; I've been there. But I promise you, if you can find a way to not live in the future, and let go of your fear and live in this moment, you are going to feel more love than you ever imagined!" She was crying. I was crying. I looked over and the saleslady was crying. "Okay, this is now the softer side of Sears!"

James and I left the store with a receipt and an installation date for my Plain Jane dryer, and as promised we stopped to listen to the band. As they hit the last note of "Heard it Through the Grapevine", the female keyboard player came running across the parking lot and straight at me.

"Is this your son?" she asked.

"Yes," I replied.

"How old is he?"

"He's four and a half," I said.

She knelt down in front of James and said, "I have a brother with Down syndrome and he is the love of my life!" Then, standing, she looked in my eyes. "Can I tell you something?" she asked.

"Um... yeah?" I stuttered, truly afraid of what was coming next.

"Look, I know how hard it is right now; I've watched my mom. But just don't live in the future, let go of your fear and live in this moment and you are going to feel more love than you ever imagined!" With that she ran back to the stage. I stood there, in disbelief. I glanced around, thinking I may be on one of those hidden camera TV shows. Two women, with the same message? Really?

Just then, I felt a tap on my shoulder. "This better be Kelly fucking Ripa!"

It was a third woman. She said, "I saw you talking with the lady in the store. Would you like to meet our special boy?"

What I wanted to say was, "No. No! Really, no thank you! I've had enough messages for today." But I followed her to her car.

She opened up the back door and there, lying across the seat on top of several pillows was what appeared to be a twelve-year-old boy. I had to hold back a gasp. He was curled up and frail and motionless. She said, "This is our son Chris. He has a rare chromosome disorder. He is blind and he can hardly speak, but he knows you're here."

She took my hand in hers and placed it on Chris' cheek. I wanted to pull away. "Chris, this is a very special mommy who has a beautiful little boy."

Then she pulled my hand to her chest and said, "They told me to put him away. But I didn't. I have taken care of him like this his whole life. He is fifty-two years old."

I'm sure the disbelief was evident on my face. Then she said, "If I could tell young mothers like yourself anything it would be this."

And I knew what was coming.

"I know how hard it is right now; I've been there. But I promise you this:

If you stop living in the future and let go of your fear and live in this moment, you are going to feel more love than you ever imagined!"

I held back the tears as much as I could. I hugged her and headed to my car. I put James in his car seat and as I turned around to back out of the parking spot, I looked at James. And for the first time in his four and a half years on this planet, I said, "I love you."

I used the rearview mirror to wipe my tears away, and for the first time I recognized who I saw, and I loved her too.

It turns out that there were actually two people in that car with special needs.

The Day I Fell in Love

> *"Inaction breeds doubt and fear. Action breeds confidence and courage. If you want to conquer fear, do not sit home and think about it. Go out and get busy."*
> *~ Dale Carnegie ~*

18.

BOB

It had been two months since my dryer broke, and since I began looking at James and life and myself differently. I came home after my experience at Sears and wrote for hours, eventually writing what would become my one-woman show. In the fall, I decided to clear out our living room and invite people to come hear my story, to see if I had something worth sharing.

One night, around two o'clock in the morning, I was awake and worried that I hadn't ordered enough klobasi, when I started flipping channels on the television. I came across an HBO documentary on a boy with Down syndrome. A camera crew had followed Brian and his family throughout the years from birth to twenty-two. They showed his successes and his failures. They showed his growth and his challenges. They interviewed his mom. And with every scene, I felt like I was watching a reality show. Then a horror pic.

At the end of the program, because obviously the story is not over, they put a graphic on the screen that read, "Brian is having a hard time adjusting to life in the real world (after high school), and still lives at home with his mother and needs constant care." The anger was instant. "I don't want this! I still can't do this!"

In the morning I told Jim through my tears that I was in fact a hypocrite and full of shit and I would not be doing the show. I mean, here I was, planning on telling everyone about my journey and about how I came to love my son, but the truth was, I still didn't want it. I still didn't want a child with Down syndrome.

Jim tried to calm me down. "Why don't you go to your happy place and just think on it for a while?" So I headed to Michaels (the craft store), by way of McDonald's.

I was standing in the floral department when this man, about sixty, approached me, holding a very ugly bunch of fake flowers. "Sorry to bother you, ma'am, but can I ask you something? What do you think of these?"

My pause and stare must have spoken volumes. But before I could answer he started crying. "You see, my wife just died. And she used to make a bouquet of flowers for our entryway every year, and I want to make one so she can see it. Will you help me?"

For the first time in a long time, I wasn't crying and I agreed to help him. I took him over to the not-so-cheap floral section and together we started making an arrangement. He told me his name was Bob. I asked him about his family and if he had support during this time. With each question, he would answer, and then break down and cry again. Finally, with the new arrangement in hand he looked at me and said, "Ma'am, I'm so sorry for crying, but some days are just harder than others." And without even thinking, before I knew what I was saying, these words came out of my mouth: "Bob, it's okay - acceptance is a daily thing."

The sentence was barely off my lips when I broke down crying. I startled him and he asked what was wrong. "Well, it's a reeeeeally long story, but I needed to say those words out loud today.

Acceptance is a daily thing.

I came home from Michaels with the answer, which was the realization that I don't need to have the answer. That there is not a Hollywood ending to this story, because the story is not over yet. It's an ongoing daily process. And some days are in fact easier than others.

I did the show in my living room and was grateful and excited that it did touch people. I laid down that night and from my bed I could see the closet window, the one that overlooks our driveway. I remembered the short bus. I remembered making the decision to stop performing. And it was not lost on me what was going on. I could almost see God with His Swiffer, pushing all the broken pieces of my career and my life and my story, into a nice neat pile. He was creating something new and beautiful out of my mess.

~

I sat in the doctor's office with James. He played with his sock monkey while I fidgeted in my chair. The doctor looked at me with the kindest eyes I had ever seen. "Lynn, I know you have been treating James with his primary diagnosis as Down syndrome, but I'm sorry to tell you that his primary diagnosis is actually autism." Her words were like fire and water and sugar all at the same time. They hurt, they wounded, they empowered and they brought relief. Because I knew it was true.

**You *believe* what you are taught or told, but
you *know* what your cells know.**

And my cells knew. I wanted to drill her with a million questions. "What are you talking about? Are you sure? How could this happen? What did I do so wrong?" But the deepest part of me knew she was right. I didn't say a word. She asked me if I needed a minute alone. I fought back the tears and said no, not wanting to appear weak. I looked at James, smiling and laughing, entertaining his overdue-for-a-washing sock monkey. But even though I knew she was right, I didn't want her to be. "I thought kids with autism bang their head on walls and do weird things with their fingers. Are you sure? Really sure?" I asked.

"Yes," she said. "Would you like me to explain what I see?" I was silent and nodded my head yes. "There are basically three areas that concern me: his minimal eye contact, the lack of imaginary play and poor social skills." With each thing she mentioned, what started inside me as a quiet 'yes' grew louder and louder. Scene after scene flashed in front of my eyes as her words played out in my head. She went on, and I listened, and I softened. And the most amazing thing happened. Instead of running, I stood still. Completely still in that horrible moment surrounded by a word I never wanted to accept — autism. Instead of hiding, I let myself be exposed. And when the mean voices showed up and told me I wasn't strong enough or capable, I hugged that that girl. And I told her, "It's okay to be afraid. I will be right here with you every step of the way."

James and I rode the elevator down to the parking garage. He made everyone inside jump up and down right before it stopped. He giggled. The other riders giggled. And I couldn't believe how much I loved the little girl inside me and my little boy.

"God comes to you disguised as your life."
~ Paula D'Arcy ~

19.

NOW

Where I'm at with God...

I was fourteen the first time I remember wondering what other people believed about God. I was walking from the duplex Karie lived in, past the Methodist church to the donut shop across the street. It was Sunday morning. I stopped and stared at the church, wondering how the people inside could believe that they were right. Didn't they know Catholisicm was the one true religion? That the Catholic Church was *the* church and they were surely going to hell? This moment of sadness for "the lost people inside" stuck with me.

Soon after, when Larry became a born again Christian, he held a family gathering in our living room with the hopes of getting our family saved. He said, "The only way you can get into heaven is to repent of your sins, profess Jesus Christ as your Lord and Savior and accept Him into your heart. It doesn't matter how much good you do or how often you go to church. If you are not born again you can not enter the kingdom of heaven." I stared at Auntie Jennie sitting across from me. I knew what Larry was saying could not be true. Especially for her.

Auntie Jennie was a saint. At least to us. When she was sixteen years old, she was crossing Stanley Avenue when her dress got caught on the bumper of a car. She was dragged over a hundred feet on her knees. The driver of the car, a local priest, never even apologized. He said he thought it was a dog, so he kept driving. Because of the accident, Auntie Jennie had to have her appendix and gall bladder removed, and she limped the rest of her life. But she kept going.

She married a handsome man named Frank and they had five children. But their lives were not easy. Their second-born, Ray, was in a gas explosion when he was five years old and suffered third-degree burns over his hands and face, scarring him for life. A few years later, their youngest son, David, who was five at the time, died of leukemia. And few years after that, Frank passed away of lung cancer. Auntie Jennie had to raise her children alone. Throughout her life she suffered from diabetes, arthritis, and lived with an aneurysm behind her aorta. And if her life hadn't been hard enough, in her eighties, she was diagnosed with breast cancer and bone cancer. And still, she kept going. Strong like bull. But here's the best part…through it all, Auntie Jennie never once complained. Never once asked, "Why me?" All she did, every single day of her life, was thank God for all of her blessings. How could—why would—a loving God send this woman to burn in hell, just because she didn't do or say or act the way someone thought she should? I didn't buy it then, and I don't buy it now. I don't believe that God, who loves us and created us, would do this to His own.

So when people ask me today, "Where are you with God?" I think of Auntie Jennie and I smile. I am at peace with my belief that God is a loving, caring God who is actively involved and living in my heart. I believe He is a part of my own soul. We are one. I believe heaven is anywhere and anytime I am with Him. And I believe hell is any separation from Him. This is my truth.

I also know that I don't have all the answers. No one knows what happens after we leave this earth. You could put any of the spiritual leaders of the past or present into a room—Gandhi, the Dalai Lama, Joseph Smith, Buddha, Billy Graham, Pope John Paul II, Oral Roberts and even my brother Larry—and they would all argue their points and try to convince each other that what they believed was the truth. That their religion was the "one true faith". But because we are all still living and breathing, it remains a mystery. And this is why it is so important to listen to your own gut.

It is in one's own spirit where truth lives.

Where I'm at with James...

I said at the beginning of this book that James was a gift; a necessary gift. And I still believe that today. He constantly provides me with the opportunity to remember what our time on this planet is supposed to be about. Living in the moment. Truth. The absence of fear. Faith. Laughter. Love. Jim always says that James was born with an extra chromosome, but it is the chromosome of love.

There are still hard times when I wish things might have turned out differently. I long for the day when James will be able to dress himself and be potty trained. But I am happy to report he started Kindergarten and he seems to love it. I still get anxious when I think about the possibility that he might only be a grocery bagger. But then I get out of my head and into my heart. I realize that all that matters is that James is happy.

I now understand that we all get something in life; some hardship that will stop us dead in our tracks: cancer, financial struggles, divorce, loss, a special needs child. No one is immune from suffering. But I also now believe this:

Being forced through misfortune allows us
to get to know our real self. You must dig,
get dirt under your fingernails, forgive what
or who got you there, to truly fall in love
with your soul.

I have a tiny bit of advice for new parents of children with special needs. Whatever it is that you love to do most, do that early with your child, and it will make life much easier. Jim decided from the beginning that James would adapt to our lives, not the other way around. So we took James on his first plane ride when he was just six weeks old and he's been on dozens since. Now he loves to fly and I'm counting the years until I can put him on a plane by himself to visit Uncle Lenny and Auntie Karie in Cleveland. We also decided early on that he would love to eat out as much as we did. Our first stop after James was released from the NICU, at only one week old, was to The Cheesecake Factory. And so today, I can take him to any restaurant, at any time, and he will sit quietly and eat his buttered noodles or French fries. He will say please and thank you and use his napkin. I kick myself every day for not using this same system when it came to getting his hair cut, potty training and visiting other people's homes. Getting him into a new place is like trying to move a mountain. We have been attempting for weeks to get James into the home of our dear friends, Steve and Susanna. We've made it to the porch swing. Hopefully we'll make it inside before winter.

Since James is mostly non-verbal, it can be frustrating to figure out what he wants. Right before he entered Kindergarten we were shocked to learn that he can spell! It seems to be the one part of his brain that is functioning on an above-average level. So whenever we can't understand him, we ask him to spell it. The other day, Jim and I were sitting on the bed and James was sitting facing us. He kept saying something we didn't understand. When we asked him to spell it, he said, "K-I-S-S."

Where I'm at with Jim...

I will quote Jim's favorite line: "Lynn and I have had thirteen wonderful years together, and we are about to celebrate our twenty-sixth wedding anniversary." We are doing life together. Sometimes we are on the same team, sometimes we are not. Sometimes he appreciates my ability and talent in operating the TV remote control and sometimes he does not. Sometimes we agree on our beliefs about spirituality, sometimes we do not. We do agree on helping James to be the best he can be, and we are committed to doing that for each other. And we absolutely, 100% agree that any fresh, gooey, carbohydrate right out of the oven is always a good thing.

Where I'm at with performing...

I made my first stage appearance at the age of five as Gretel in a local production of *The Sound of Music*. This began a love affair with theater and the ability to share stories in front of a live audience. But my journey did not take me down that road, even though I still had a burning desire. Which is why Psalm 37:4 is my second favorite scripture: "Delight yourself in the Lord, and he will give you the desires of your heart." (International Standard Version)

I am so grateful and thankful to God and the universe for taking what I thought was a dying career and transforming it into something even more beautiful. Of course, this couldn't have happened until I released my controlling death grip on everything.

Faith is handing over to God everything you are, have, and hope for, along with all the parts you've screwed up, knowing that She is going to a better job with all of it than you ever did.

After my dryer broke, and after doing the show in our living room, we were able to take the one-woman production of *Wrap Your*

Heart Around It to stages in New York, Los Angeles, Nashville and even to Poland, and I look forward to seeing where it appears next. People often ask, "But did you quit playing polka?" That's like asking if I quit eating sugar.

Where I'm at with depression...

Depression isolates, so I surround myself with friends and family and Lexapro.

Where I'm at with alcohol and codependency...

I love a good passion fruit cocktail. But I understand that some people can have a drink occasionally and others cannot.

Lenny, Karie & Me, NYC, 2011

So, like the alcoholic who can not even have one sip, I've learned enough to know now that I can not let the slightest codependent thought take root in my head. The bad news is that I will have to do this for the rest of my life. It may get easier with time and wisdom, but I will always be in recovery. The good news is that I no longer believe this to be a problem, but rather a process.

> ## Life is not a series of challenges to be overcome, but situations to awaken to, accept and experience.

Where I'm at with sugar...

The HOT NOW light is on, so I must go.

Stay tuned...

About the Author

The definition of talent is, "A natural ability to do something well," which perfectly describes LynnMarie Rink. However, it seems as if she is one of the lucky ones, born with the natural ability to do many things well.

LynnMarie is a five-time Grammy nominated performing artist. Her style of music, played on a unique instrument called a diatonic button accordion, has garnered her worldwide attention, as well as an appearance on *The Tonight Show with Jay Leno*. She has performed all over the world and collaborated with some of the music industry's most respected artists like Chet Atkins, Hal Ketchum, Dobie Gray, Air Supply and Vince Gill.

When she is not performing on stage in front of the cameras, she is working behind the scenes as a television associate director and producer. "I work in television to support my music habit," laughs LynnMarie, but she has made quite a name for herself. Producing and assistant directing such high profile shows as *The Academy of Country Music Awards Red Carpet for GAC*, live music shows from the Super

Bowl for CMT, and a variety of shows for dick clark productions, her day job provides just as much excitement and intrigue as her music career.

That leaves her spare time, which she recently spent by writing and starring in her own off-Broadway production of her life story, *Wrap Your Heart Around It*, produced by Emmy-winning director Paul Miller. She performed the musical dramedy in front of sold-out audiences in New York City, and was awarded "Best New Production" by the United Solo Theatre Festival. She followed up that success with a six-week run at the Falcon Theatre in Burbank, about which the LA Times said, "Rink's unforced warmth and affecting candor amounts to a one-woman love bomb. Perhaps not since Mona Golabek's *The Pianist of Willesden Lane* has Los Angeles witnessed so genuinely inspirational a personal memoir. I dare you not to wrap your heart around it."

Currently, LynnMarie can be found sharing her story of hope and encouragement as a motivational entertainer and public speaker for women's groups, conferences and special needs organizations.

LynnMarie lives in Nashville, Tennessee, with her husband Jim and their son James.